Attack!

Michael Hardcastle used to be a journalist with a daily newspaper, and now contributes to a number of magazines. He has written more than eighty books for young people, many of them about football and other sports. He says his own playing career at school was 'completely undistinguished', but he has loyally supported the same team since he was eleven. He lives in Yorkshire.

Also in Armada, featuring Mark Fox:

The First Goal
Breakaway
On the Ball
Shooting Star
Goal in Europe
Kick Off

Attack!

A Mark Fox Story

Michael Hardcastle

AN ORIGINAL ARMADA

Attack! was first published in the U.K. in
Armada in 1982
by Fontana Paperbacks,
14 St. James's Place, London SW1A 1PS.

Printed in Great Britain by
Love & Malcomson Ltd.,
Brighton Road, Redhill, Surrey.

Chapter One

'Go on, attack!' Mark Fox called.

He was watching the boy with the thin legs. Although the boy didn't look particularly athletic because he was so slightly built, and Mark feared he wouldn't be much good at resisting a tackle, in terms of footballing ability the dark-haired youngster was far ahead of the rest of the group of first-year pupils at Hedger's School that Mark had been asked to coach

As another player completely missed his kick when the ball bounced in front of him, Mark sighed and blew a long blast on his whistle. Every boy stopped dead as if he'd been shot.

'Well, at least you play to the whistle if nothing else,' Mark observed. 'But at your age you really ought to be able to manage a bit more than that. Didn't any of you play in an organised team before you came to this school? What about you?' He gestured at the thin-legged boy. 'You look as if you've got *some* idea of what to do with the ball.'

'I *wanted* to get into the team in the village where I live but all the players are a couple of years older than me and they wouldn't give me a chance,' was the reply. 'So, mostly, I've just practised with an old tennis ball on my own. That's better than nothing.'

'That's right!' exclaimed Mark, brightening. 'That's just how I started – training with a small ball, I mean. If you can control that then you can usually master the bigger ball. So – very good. What's your name?'

'Karl Jenson.'

'O.K., then, I think we'd better get down to some basics and Karl here can help me to demonstrate them. If you don't master these then you'll have no chance whatsoever of making progress as soccer players,' Mark told them. Now, at last, some of the boys were paying attention. 'Right, Karl, we'll start with passing a ball, just using the inside of the foot. That way you can *steer* the ball where you want it to go. Never, repeat never, use the toe-cap. We'll try it from the stationary position first, then on the move.'

The coaching idea had come from Ted Bayley, the sports master at Hedger's. Now that Mark had played for the Reserves' team of a First Division club, the sports master felt that the school as a whole should be given the chance to benefit from Mark's knowledge and experience of professional soccer. So he had arranged for Mark to take charge of a variety of coaching sessions to be held at intervals throughout the term. Mark, as a senior pupil, was allowed to take the sessions on his own without a teacher in attendance. 'In that way, Ted Bayley pointed out, 'you can please yourself what kind of skills you teach and *how* you teach 'em. All I'll do is drop in now and again and see how you're getting on. I'll just act as a consultant, if you like.'

Although Mr Bayley had set up the scheme before asking his new coach for his co-operation, Mark had initially been in favour of it. Soon, however, it proved to be an irritation: many of the sessions had been in after-school hours when Mark would rather have been doing something else. Others were held during the midday break when he preferred to play table tennis with some of his friends. But most of all, the general low level of ability of so many of those he was trying to coach had begun to depress him. And he would rather have been practising his own skills than encouraging others to develop them.

As an Associated Schoolboy with a First Division club, he felt he needed as much practice as possible. His ambition, of course, was one day to become a professional in the Athletic first team.

Now, as the bunch of first formers struggled to master one or two fundamental techniques, Mark glanced yet again at his watch. Another full minute, he decided, and that would be it: he'd signal the end of the training spell. Officially, it should last another ten minutes, but he really didn't think he could maintain interest as long as that even if the youngsters could. They'd had twenty minutes and that was surely long enough for anyone. In any case, it was twenty minutes of his own free time he'd sacrificed.

By now, Karl Jenson was giving free rein to his own talents on the ball. Since Mark had praised his attitude to training, he was seizing the opportunity to show what he could do with the ball; switching the ball from foot to foot to evade lunging tackles from his fellows; dribbling at speed; turning complete circles and taking the ball round with him by using only the outside of his boot; and, finally, flicking it up on to a toe and from there to a knee. It was an exceptional performance and Mark couldn't fail to be impressed. He made a mental note to draw Ted Bayley's attention to the boy's abilities. Even if Karl was only eleven, it might still be possible to play him in one of the school's junior sides. Mark himself had at one time been the youngest member of the school team that took part in county events: in such games size mattered but sheer skill was more important.

'Pretty good, that, Karl,' Mark called out to him. 'If you can turn it on like that in a match you'll definitely have a future in the game.'

'Thanks – Mark,' the boy replied shyly.

'Right, lads, I think we'll call it a day,' Mark went on. He sounded, he realised, like the official trainer at any professional club. 'But next time we have a session I hope to see a lot of improvement in ball control and passing. If you *want* to be a good soccer player then you've got to do some training on your own whenever you've got a free minute. And the smaller the ball you use, well, the better you'll be. O.K., off you go.'

Some sprinted away, others strolled because they were genuinely tired at the end of a school day. Two hardly moved at all until Mark did: and then they fell into step beside him. Predictably, one was Karl Jenson. The other, Peter Whelton, was Karl's friend and one of the poorest footballers in the group, but one who was desperately keen to improve.

'Will you be playing for Athletic Reserves on Saturday?' Karl asked in a very tentative manner.

'Er, maybe,' Mark replied cautiously. He hadn't played well in his previous game and he suspected he might be rested this week. At the club it was the policy not to use the word 'dropped' when teams were chosen. 'I won't know until the team-sheet is posted up on Friday. That's the way all the players learn whether they're in a team or not.'

'Oh.'

That was all Karl said for a moment, and Mark supposed the younger boy was just making polite conversation as they returned to the main building from the sports field. But Karl went on, 'Sometimes, you see, Peter and I come to watch you play – well, I mean we both support Athletic. We're just praying for the day when Athletic win the First Division title.'

'Oh, I see,' Mark said, undeniably flattered by their interest in his association with the football club. 'Well, I suppose I could get you a couple of complimentary tickets for the game if that's what you want. If you call at—'

'Oh no!' they exclaimed simultaneously, looking as shocked as they sounded. 'We *weren't* asking for free tickets, honestly,' Karl continued. 'It's just that, well, I've always wanted to have a look round the *inside* of a real football club – and so has Pete. You know, the dressing-rooms, the big bath, the treatment room, the place where they keep all the gear – oh, everything there is to see. So we were just wondering, well, whether there was any chance at all that you could fix it up for us.'

Mark grinned. 'Yeah, I reckon so. I had the same sort of ambition when I was your age – but I didn't achieve it for a long time. Look, I'll have a word with Buzz Burton, the guy who's in charge of the Reserves. He'll know what can be fixed up for you. O.K.?'

'Fantastic! Thanks very much, Mark.'

They were within a few strides of the main building, and Mark was about to say that he'd get them tickets for Saturday's match anyway, when Ted Bayley came hurrying round a corner, and stopped dead when he caught sight of them. The expression on the sports master's face was hard to interpret but Mark knew that something had displeased him. It could be anything, for Ted Bayley was an unpredictable character.

'Something wrong?' inquired Mark.

'Should something be wrong?' the sports master asked, with raised eyebrows.

This time Mark was silent. He'd been involved in arguments before with Ted Bayley, whose sarcasm was renowned among older pupils. It was generally believed that Ted had to get his own back on somebody because he had troubles at home; and the boys he taught were the nearest, and easiest, victims.

Karl Jenson and his friend had also come to a halt and now, nervously, they looked from Mark to the teacher and back again. Mr Bayley often gave the impression that he could find a terrible fault where none existed.

'You two, get off home,' he snapped, to their great relief. 'Don't hang about and risk a severe chill after a *long* and *hard* training session.'

'Yes, sir!' They sprinted for the cover of the changing rooms.

Bayley waited until the first formers were out of sight before he spoke again. Mark sensed that another row was brewing. He waited, chewing at the inside of his lower lip.

'They're your favourites, those two, are they?' Bayley asked to his great surprise.

'Of course not! They were just asking me something, that's all. One of them – Karl Jenson, the thin lad – shows a lot of ability. Could be quite good one day if he gets the right sort of encouragement.'

'You should know, Mark, that I don't approve of the idea of any teacher – or instructor – having *favourites*, especially where team games are concerned,' Mr Bayley went on as if Mark had not spoken. 'I've always believed that the game is greater than the individual. You know that.'

'Yes,' said Mark, non-committally. He had heard that phrase used dozens of times during his years at the school and had become thoroughly sick of it. Nor had he forgotten the way in which Ted Bayley had deliberately been severe on him at times as if to prove his point; for no one else at Hedger's School had achieved the same sort of soccer success as Mark Fox.

'Right,' Bayley resumed briskly. 'Now, what really puzzles me is why you've finished this coaching session so early – a good ten minutes early, by my reckoning. Were you bored, perhaps?'

'Er, no,' Mark muttered. But now he really did feel guilty. Bored was exactly what he felt towards the end of training.

'Well, then, what was the reason? I thought I was being generous in giving you a free hand to coach in the way you think fit. But that didn't include the freedom to vary the times of the sessions to suit your own convenience.'

'I wasn't doing! It was just that, well, I thought they'd done enough, that's all. Apart from young Karl, there isn't much talent among that lot.'

'All the more reason, I should have thought, for you to try and *help* them to improve. Cutting the time down won't achieve any results, will it?'

Mark didn't answer. He knew he had no chance of

winning this argument or even getting out of it with honour. He might as well let Talking Ted make it game, set and match as quickly as possible.

'Very well,' Bayley continued, believing he'd sorted that one out. 'Now, to Saturday's match, which is vital.'

There he paused and waited for Mark's reaction. Could it possibly be, Mark wondered, that the sports master was going to ask for a ticket to attend the Reserves match?

'Er, what about the match?' Mark asked cautiously. 'We're playing Wolves in the Central League, you know.'

'Athletic Reserves are playing Wolves in the Central League, you mean,' said Ted formally. 'The school, and that includes YOU, are playing Kelmington High in the second round of the Wrigley Cup. An away fixture, as you know.'

'What!' Mark exploded. 'That's not on Saturday! No date's been fixed for it since Kelmington had to cry off because of the 'flu virus they all went down with – and, anyway, they wouldn't play it on Saturday. That's a crazy idea!'

'Crazy it may be to you, Fox, but not to everybody else. I've just had a phone call from Mr Ridgefield at Kelmington. He's been checking on the rules of the competition again and discovered that if the organising secretary doesn't have the names of the second round winners by next Monday those teames which haven't completed their ties will be eliminated. Mr Ridgefield and I are of the same mind: that's not going to happen to us. The only available date for the tie is Saturday – so Saturday it will be.'

'But we could play straight after school one evening if it's as urgent as that! I mean —'

'No we couldn't, for a whole variety of reasons that are no concern of yours. Now, on Thursday I propose to hold a training and tactical meeting that —'

'But why didn't YOU know about the Monday deadline?' Mark demanded. 'You're just as much involved in dates and things as the Kelmington lot!'

'This happens to be a brand new schools competition, as you well know. Sometimes organisers don't always make the conditions as clear as they ought to be. But that's all beside the point, Mark. Instead of protesting about the choice of date, you, as the captain of the school team, should automatically be thinking about how the tie is to be won, so that Hedger's can go on to collect the Cup. If this is going to be your last season with us it would be nice to have something to show for it. I should have thought you might have looked at it in that light, too.'

All Mark could think about at that moment was what the effect might be on his career with Athletic if he missed out on the game with Wolves' Reserves. Someone from the third team would take his place, would probably play a blinder and . . .

'Look, what time has this Cup match been fixed for?' he asked desperately. Maybe there was a chance he could play in both games.

'I know just waht you're thinking, young Fox, but you can forget it,' was Mr Bayley's stern rejoinder. 'When the school agreed to allow you to sign for Athletic as an Associated Achoolboy it was made very plain to you that school matches would always – *always*

– take precedence over playing for Athletic. You signed the form and you know what it says. I'm also aware that Gareth Blake, Athletic's manager, told you the same thing. I think it's time you remembered that you're still a boy at Hedger's School, you're not a professional footballer *yet*. You can forget all about what Athletic Reserves are doing on Saturday. You'll be playing for your school – and you'll play as well as you know how. No sulks, no snide comments, no feigned injuries or anything like that. Is that clearly understood?'

'Yes – sir.' Mark made his answer as formal as possible. Inwardly, he was seething.

'Good, I'm glad you're being sensible about it. I know how impetuous you can be and I wouldn't want the Head to have to take any disciplinary action against you at this stage of your career. That would be rather humiliating, don't you think?'

'It'll be humiliating to have to tell them at Athletic that I can't turn out for the Reserves because I can't get away from school,' Mark muttered.

'Well, that's your problem, if it IS a problem,' was the unsympathetic comment. 'Seems pretty straightforward to me but then I don't have *divided* loyalties. There's only *one* team I'm committed to, the team I'd like to see win something before it's too late.'

Mark knew what Bayley meant by that. The present Hedger's team was probably the best to represent the school in its history; but soon, when Mark left and a couple of other players moved to a sixth form college, it would start to break up. In recent seasons the team had done well without actually achieving any honours. The worst disappointment had been the defeat by Zeeland

Comprehensive in the Final of the County Schools' Knock-Out Cup. It had taken Ted Bayley a very long time to get over that disaster. Mark himself, however, had had the compensation shortly afterwards of playing for England Juniors in a summer international tournament in Switzerland.

But at this moment all he could think of was who would be taking his place in the Athletic team on Saturday, and, worse, still, whether Buzz Burton would start to forget about him if he couldn't turn out regularly for the Reserves.

Chapter Two

Mark sat at the back of the coach that was taking the Hedger's school team the thirty-odd miles to Kelmington. For once he didn't take in the attractive countryside through which they were passing, or get involved in the noisy conversations of the rest of the team. He wondered gloomily what his Athletic team-mates were doing at that moment – and whether any of them really minded that he wasn't there. Buzz Burton had been sympathetic but brief when Mark had rung to say he couldn't turn out. Mark wished he could persuade himself that the coach had sounded disappointed.

His attention was jolted into the present by the sudden braking of the coach-driver, as a black dog, chased by an irate child, shot across the road in front of them. The passengers were thrown forward and one boy bumped his head against a seat, the driver blew a long breath of relief and rolled his eyes skywards – and the dog escaped the wrath of the child as well as the front wheels of the coach.

'Hope that's the *worst* thing that happens to us today,' remarked Bobby Storr, the goalkeeper.

'The worst thing that'll happen will be what we'll do to you, Bobby, if you let in any goals and we lose,' promised Jerry Rendell, a speedy right-winger and one of the oldest members of the team. He had a streak of violence in his make-up and the threat to Bobby was not entirely casual. Jerry had dreamed for years of winning a medal and he'd decided that the Wrigley Cup was his very best chance of picking it up.

'Having a black dog run across your path is supposed to be lucky, though, isn't it?' said Justin Greene, one of the strikers, who was sitting at the front and almost alongside the driver.

'That's *cats*, you nut!' Bobby told him exasperatedly. 'You talk more rubbish than anybody I know.'

Mark put in, 'Mason Smith – you know, the former Scotland international at Athletic – well, he believes that if he sees a wedding on the day he's backed a horse, then that horse has no chance of winning. But if he sees a funeral then he's bound to be on a winner. Jimmy Terndale reckons Mason believes the same thing about a vital match but he won't admit it. Anyway, he always has his head stuck in a newspaper on a coach journey to a match so he won't catch a glimpse of a wedding.'

By now his school team-mates were used to Mark's references to events and personalities at Athletic F.C. Most of them were somewhat awed by the familiarity

Mark possessed with professional players they watched from the terraces or read about in national papers. They enjoyed hearing interesting bits of gossip about the Athletic staff and so they always listened when Mark had something to tell them. Yet, because he moved in such exalted circles these days, the majority of them no longer felt any real kinship with Mark Fox. He was their captain, but not by their choice; the job had been given to him by Ted Bayley because the sports master believed that it would encourage Mark to give 'his all,' as he put it, for the team and not for his own glory.

'I don't think we want to be talking about luck,' Ted Bayley now said heavily. 'And it's just morbid to go on about funerals. Anyway, they don't usually hold funerals on a Saturday so that's senseless talk.'

He paused as if giving Mark an opportunity to challenge him. Mark, however, had no intention of getting into another argument.

'No, we've got to win our games by ability, by real *talent* and determination and *character*,' he went on in a fairly familiar vein. His pep talks didn't vary much from season to season and he scarcely ever indulged in tactical discussions. His favourite words were the ones he'd just used: character and determination. Ted Bayley seemed to believe they were the answer to every situation. Only occasionally at half-time did he make some comment of a tactical nature: and even then the team were left to interpret it for themselves.

Mark wasn't listening. His mind had drifted back from Athletic F.C. affairs to the forthcoming game. Hedger's had not met Kelmington before in any sort of competition, so their oppopnents were completely unknown quantities. Ted Bayley claimed he'd tried to make some enquiries of his opposite number, Mr Ridgefield, but they hadn't unearthed much. None of the Kelmington players had been selected for representative games so far as anyone at Hedger's knew; and the team hadn't, apparently, made any impact on the league in which it played.

Well, Mark decided eventually, their ignorance about the opposition wouldn't matter much once the game was under way. The intention must be to attack as hard and as often as possible from the start and score the goals that would put the result of the tie beyond doubt. That was the only way to play a knock-out cup match.

It was about time, he reflected, that he scored a few goals himself. So far that season, they'd been in fairly short supply. And when he wasn't scoring goals regularly Mark tended to fret. He could explain away his lack of recent success in front of goal easily enough: he had been playing against some of the best defences in the Central League, the competition in which Athletic Reserves participated. Moreover, he hadn't had a settled partnership with another striker: team changes in the Reserves had been frequent for all manner of reasons and so Mark hadn't been able to build a relationship, or even reach a clear understanding about different roles, with any player in the team. So he could comfort himself with the thought that the playing styles of his tem-mates at Hedger's were fairly predictable. In the past two or three seasons there had been remarkably few major changes because many of the players had been introduced into the side at a young age. Justin

Greene was the latest example of Ted Bayley's willingness to give younger boys a chance if they seemed to have the ability. Mark had an idea that, before long, he and Justin would combine really well up front, especially when Jackie Newland was in top form and pushing the ball through at the right moment. Jackie was both a good ball-winner in midfield and an inspirational playmaker at times: but, in Mark's opinion, he faded out of the game when things weren't going well for him.

'. . . sticking a few away yourself, eh, Mark?'

'Oh, er, sorry, what did you say, Boss?'

'I was saying to you, while you were dreaming, that I trusted you would be sticking a few goals away yourself in this match.'

'Oh, sure, that's *exactly* what I was thinking,' Mark replied with a grin. He could tell that Ted Bayley didn't believe him for a moment: but he also knew that when the sports master started to use current soccer jargon he was in a reasonably good mood.

'Well, then, make sure you live up to your ambitions – for the sake of the school, if nothing else,' added Ted, determined as usual to have the last word on any matter. He felt it didn't do any harm to demonstrate to the other boys that he didn't treat Mark Fox with any special favour on team occasions.

'But even if you don't score another goal all season, Teddy-boy can't drop you, can he, Mark?' whispered Brian Torson, who was occupying the next seat. Brian, who had a Danish father, was arguably the fastest player in the team after Mark and usually they operated as wing partners. Mark had hopes that one day Brian would be good enough to play for a professional club.

'Don't be too sure about *that*!' Mark responded in a similarly low tone. 'Ted would love to kick me out of the team – and he'd do it on the flimsiest excuse. He's always had this funny love-hate attitude to good players. I reckon it's because he's jealous. He never achieved anything in his life – you know, as a sportsman – so he resents those who do. My Grandad – the one who used to be a professional player – he says lots of sports teachers are like that. Quite a lot of soccer coaches, too, who never made the top grade. Amazing, isn't it, how small-minded some people can be?'

Before Brian could make another comment, the coach swept through some impressive wrought-iron gates, and came to a halt in front of an ivy-covered building that looked more like a stately home than a school.

The appearance of the place silenced everyone else, too, for a few moments. Then Jackie Newland, who had a fondness for watching on television old films about high society, asked: 'Hey, do you think they have a butler to serve the meals and footmen to carry messages from classroom to classroom? Maybe the Head's Lord Smith-hyphen-Jones or something!'

'If they've got footmen then I hope they've a spare one to clean my boots!' exclaimed Justin Greene.

As the players clambered out of the coach a tall, slim young man in a light-coloured suit came out of the front entrance to greet them. To their great surprise he made a point of shaking each one of them by the hand and welcoming them to Kelmington High School. He sincerely hoped, he said, they would enjoy their visit. Their astonishment grew when they learned that he was Barry Ridgefield, the sports master. He looked, as Brian Torson observed, more like an assistant bank manager than a teacher specialising in sport. The contrast between him and Ted Bayley, who regularly wore an old track suit which did not hide his middle-age spread, was extreme.

'I'll show you to your dressing-room,' Mr Ridgefield was saying smoothly to a bemused-looking Ted Bayley. 'I'm sure you'll find it contains everything you may need, but if anything is lacking then I shall be on hand to see to it. I have also pinned up our team-sheet, though I don't expect any of the names will mean anything to you.'

'Well, er, thank you very much – I'm sure everything will be fine,' said Bayley, feeling that he must say something.

'Oh yes, one thing I forgot,' Mr Ridgefield added. 'We shall, naturally, be entertaining you to some refreshments after the match. Just something to save you the trouble and expense of stopping for a meal on the way home.'

As the team trooped along the corridor towards the changing-rooms the comments about Kelmington's style and hospitality were fired off like machine-gun bullets. This, they felt, was going to be an experience they wouldn't forget.

'Isn't it great of them to lay on a banquet for us?' Jerry Rendell inquired of anyone who would listen. 'I mean, it'll be a bit like Wembley where the winners celebrate with champagne and salmon and chips at a very big party afterwards. Still, we'll deserve it, the way we're going to play. I might even feel a bit mean about scoffing all their grub after pounding their defence to pieces!'

The dressing-room, reached by what seemed to be a very roundabout route, was in a modern block and couldn't have been more up-to-date: the shower units, as Bobby Storr remarked, were in the luxury class. As someone who could get very chilled during a match through sheer inactivity at his end, Bobby especially appreciated a hot shower. The windows were, inevitably, of frosted glass and so there was no glimpse to be had of the pitch.

'If they can provide this for visitors I wonder what their own set-up's like,' went on Jerry, who was totally relishing the atmosphere. 'Bet it's not a lot better at Athletic, is it, Mark?'

'Well, I wouldn't say that,' Mark replied cautiously. 'But I've been in dressing-rooms at other professional clubs that aren't in this class, I can tell you. I remember one of the players at Athletic saying that if a club's got really good facilities the odds are it'll have a good team as well.'

'Yeah, but that's just for professionals, isn't it? I mean, noboddy's ever heard of this lot, have they? You don't recognise any name on the team-sheet, do you? Nobody you've played with – or against – in county youth matches?'

Mark let his eyes run down the list of names pinned on an official-looking notice board just inside the door. Then he shook his head. None of them meant anything to him.

'One of 'em seems to be foreign,' Jerry pointed out. 'Dalechamps, that's not English, is it? Looks like he'll be operating in midfield.'

Ted Bayley had recovered by now from the various surprises that had come his way. It was time, he decided, to remind his team of what was expected of them when the match began.

'I don't think we have to worry too much about the opposition. If we play well enough then they'll be doing the worrying – about *us*. A good start is essential in any cup match, so I want to see Hedger's on the attack from the outset. An early goal can make all the difference.

'So, when you see the whites of the goalie's eyes, have a shot – at the net, I mean, not at the goalie himself!'

Most of the boys had heard this joke too often to react. Ted frowned, tightened his lips and turned to his own goalkeeper.

'Storr, I want an especially cool display from you. I don't want to see any loose punching. Your hands are to hold the ball with, not to punch it like a demented boxer. It really is about time you eradicated that weakness. Understand, Robert?'

Bobby, who hated to be addressed as Robert by anyone, looked pained.

'I only punch by instinct – and all top goalies rely on instinct. It's what makes a goalie. Under pressure, the main thing is to get the ball away, isn't it?'

'Just remember what I've said,' Bayley said heavily.

Mark glanced at the sports master with a new sense of respect. Until then he hadn't realised that Ted was aware of Bobby Storr's weakness. On several occasions Bobby had endangered Hedger's defence by missing the ball altogether or directing it straight at an opponent while attempting to punch it clear.

When he pulled on his team's light blue shirt Mark

wondered what colour Kelmington favoured; he hoped it didn't match Athletic's black-and-white stripes. He could do without regular reminders that he might so easily have been playing for the Reserves in the match at Leeside Park.

In fact, the home side was wearing an all-red strip – and a rather dazzling red at that. But it was the pitch, not the opposition, that was the focus of attention for the Hedger's players when they left the dressing-room and followed the referee down a narrow, hedge-lined lane behind the school buildings.

'Lord, it's got a slope on it like Mount Everest!' exclaimed Jackie Newland.

The incline ran diagonally, from one corner flag to another, and the fall could definitely be measured in metres.

'Well, I certainly don't fancy running up *that* in the second half,' Mark remarked to Justin Greene. 'So I hope I win the toss! We can give the defence a helping hand if necessary and then really turn it on in the second half. That's when Cup-ties are usually won.'

'Have you never thought of getting this field levelled?' Ted Bayley asked his opposite number. He was as astonished as his team by the gradient and he suspected it was bound to give Kelmington an unfair advantage. 'I mean, it hardly seems fit for a fair test of football skill.'

Ridgefield managed to look genuinely puzzled. 'Do you mean you don't know about our slope? Well, I am surprised, Mr Bayley. I mean, I thought it was quite famous – almost as famous as Yeovil's.'

'We haven't met any team who's played here, so the

word doesn't seem to have got round our circles,' Bayley told him.

'Well, of course, it doesn't really make much difference. After all, it is the same for both teams. Still, I'm sorry you weren't advised about it. Slipped my mind completely when we were chatting on the phone.' Ridgefield paused and then added with a hint of a smile: 'Still, you didn't say anything about having a semi-professional in your side, did you? Must make a vast difference to your boys to have someone of his experience and skills to rely on.'

'Mark Fox, you mean? He's not a *professional* – not yet, anyway, though he seems to think it's just a formality. He's only an Associated Schoolboy with Athletic. I'm not at all sure he possesses quite the true character to get through to the top in professional sport.'

Barry Ridgefield made no immediate reply to that and, a moment later, both men started to stroll along the touchline as the teams completed their shooting-in practice and the referee summoned the captains to toss up.

'That's a foreign player you've got in the side, is it?' remarked Ted, though he hadn't yet spotted anyone who might not be English. 'Dalechamps, I think the name is, according to your team-sheet.'

'Ah yes, that's right. He's French – father's a mining engineer and the family cames from Lyons. M. Dalechamps is working over here on some EEC project and the family came with him as the job is likely to last a couple of years or so. Jean-Paul – that's him, the stocky, dark-haired lad over there – is quite a useful player in a midfield role. Works very hard at his game and is most enthusiastic.' Ridgefield paused, then added, 'Oh, I see they're changing ends, so your team is, er, going to have the slope in its favour in the second half. Well, as they always say, may the better team win!'

Kelmington had the support of scores of pupils as well as a surprising number of adults, and Ted Bayley was made aware the moment the match kicked-off that Hedger's would feel the disadvantage of being the away team. The volume of noise in favour of Kel-ming-ton was immense.

With such vocal encouragement and the slope in their favour from the outset it was inevitable that the team in red should launch an immediate attack. Dalechamps was in possession from the kick-off and he surged through the middle, easily holding off every attempt to tackle him. Even Jackie Newland bounced off the French boy as if he'd made contact with a rubber ball. Then, when it seemed that weight of numbers must succeed where everything else had failed, Dalechamps switched the play to the right wing with a gem of a pass.

The winger retained the ball just long enough to outwit the full-back and then crossed it with accuracy and speed. Kelmington's tall striker headed it back instead of towards goal – a ploy that non-plussed Perrett, the boy who was trying to mark him. The ball fell perfectly for Dalechamps, who hadn't stopped running, to try a shot. It was, as even Ted Bayley had to admit, a screamer.

Bobby Storr didn't even see the ball as it went past him into the roof of the net.

On the touchline some of the younger children from

the village actually turned cart-wheels to express their joy at such a goal.

There was a glazed look in Bobby's eyes as he retrieved the ball and booted it up the middle. Mark Fox was speechless. Not a single Hedger's player had touched the ball from the kick-off and the goal had been scored in a matter of a few seconds. None of his team-mates was at fault (they'd hardly had a chance to be!); it was simply the sheer speed of Kelmington's attack that had put them in the lead.

Within a minute, Kelmington had doubled that lead. This time, Dalechamps parted with the ball quite quickly after receiving it from a team-mate who'd intercepted Mark's pass to Brian Torson. But Dalechamps clamoured for the return pass – and got it. With minimal effort he then hoisted it down the middle. Perret mis-judged the bounce on that slope – the ball seemed to him to gather top-spin as it came off the well-grassed surface – and Kelmington's striker raced past him to gain possession.

The boy was as fast as he was tall – and plainly he had a good temperament. He displayed no sign of panic as Bobby Storr rushed out from goal.

The striker judged his moment well. As the goalkeeper committed himself to a headlong dive, he steered the ball past him, aiming for a spot just inside the far upright. Bobby fell in a heap and clutched only grass.

The ball, inevitably affected by the slope, veered off course fractionally and rebounded from the post in front of the open goal. Hedger's right back was the only one in a position to reap the benefit from that slice of bad luck for Kelmington. He had been sprinting back to give cover and now, arriving in the right place at the critical moment, he toe-ended the ball over the dead-ball line for a corner. He might have been able to do better than that, and clear the ball completely, but it was enough for him that he'd prevented the goal. Bobby, trying to recover his own lost dignity, patted him on the back as he took up his place for the corner-kick on the right.

That kick was taken, left-footed, by Dalechamps. It was well-flighted and when Perrett went up for the in-swinging ball he was challenged by Kelmington's lofty striker; it was the latter who rose the higher and, getting his forehead to the ball, he nodded it to a team-mate. As the ball dropped, the Hedger's defenders seemed to be transfixed. No one offered a challenge as the Kelmington player struck the ball sweetly on the volley to send it rocketing into the net for a second spectacular goal. Dalechamps, arms spread wide to embrace the scorer, rushed in to lead the celebrations that continued all the way back to the centre circle.

'Why didn't you tackle the guy?' Bobby Storr was screaming at his defenders; and they, in their turn, were searching for other culprits to blame.

Mark knew that some of the responsibility for the disaster was his. The move that had led to the corner had come about because of his weak pass from midfield to Brian Torson. He had more or less given the ball away at a moment when possession was important. Hedger's had needed to recover their composure after going a goal down right at the start of the match. Now, they were in deep trouble.

'Come on, stick at it, we're still in the game!' he

yelled, clapping his hands to get the attention of his players. A leader had to say something, however banal, at a time of crisis.

Ted Bayley could think of nothing at all to say. What none of his team knew was that Ted was looking for another job. He wanted a post with more responsibility in a bigger, and more fashionable, school. So far he'd had no success at all with the teams he'd trained. But if the present Hedger's side could win the Wrigley Cup then he'd have something to show for his years at the school. It would prove that he produced winners. At an interview for a top job it would be a trump card for him to play.

Now, it looked as though the team was going to be swept out of the event almost before this second round match had begun. Ted Bayley felt sick.

'All about taking your chances, this game, isn't it?' asked a cheerful voice at his side. He hadn't even been aware of the arrival of Barry Ridgefield, now looking understandably smug.

'That's right,' Ted muttered through clenched teeth.

'Still, there's a long way to go yet – so anything can happen,' Ridgefield went on. He didn't sound, though, as if he quite believed that. He sounded like a man who knew he was on a winner.

What Ted Bayley was thinking now was that Ridgefield's description of the French boy as 'quite a useful player in midfield' was the under-statement of the sporting year. Jean-Paul was all too plainly the possessor of great talent for the game of soccer. He couldn't imagine how Hedger's were going to shackle him so that they might have a ghost of a chance of getting back into this match.

'Look, we've got to retain possession as long as possible,' Mark was saying urgently at that moment to his first lieutenant, Jackie Newland. 'If we can slow it down and just push the ball around we can start to take charge. But another goal'll kill us off.'

So, after kicking off again, Mark turned the ball back to Jackie and immediately edged out towards the left flank. Jackie screened the ball well as a Kelmington player tried to harry him into letting it go: and then Hedger's midfielder neatly chipped it over an opponent's head as he sent it out to the wing. Mark came back to pick it up, held off a couple of tackles and then, by pre-arrangement, back-heeled the ball to Brian. And Brian, in turn, eventually slid it back to Jackie Newland. Hedger's were playing the triangle of possession.

All too soon, however, Kelmington, roared on by their devout followers, returned to the attack. A throw-in was wasted when the home side's left-winger darted forward to intercept the ball and then hook it fiercely into the middle. The ubiquitous Dalechamps chested the ball down, spun, twisted and then surged forward down the slope. Mark, who'd been deliberately loitering in midfield, attempted a tackle and succeeded only in catching the French boy's ankle. Dalechamps collapsed dramatically and lay ominously still.

The referee, a bulky and very tall man, blew immediately for a foul. As he raced past Mark he gave him a stern look but didn't say anything. He had recognised that it was an accident. The crowd, however, were not so tolerant. Their favourite player had been felled and they showed their disapproval with shrill whistles and an assortment of jeers. Ted Bayley looked surprised. He thought that such a well-appointed school would have a civilised fan club.

It turned out to be a track-suited physiotherapist, not sports master Barry Ridgefield, who sprinted on to the pitch to administer treatment to the prone French boy. The sponge, aided by a spray and inhaler, duly worked its magic. So Dalechamps was soon on his feet again, to the obvious relief of his team-mates.

The free kick had been pumped into the visitors' penalty area and Bobby Storr very nearly made a hash of it when the ball came to him at head height. His juggling act brought a challenge from a striker who tried to hook the ball over Bobby's head into the net. Although Mark felt that such a move constituted dangerous play, the referee didn't agree with him and no action was taken against the striker.

For the next few minutes the pressure on Hedger's defence was virtually incessant and on two or three occasions Kelmington were decidedly unlucky not to add to their score. They were, as Mark noted, a much heavier, altogether brawnier, side than Hedger's. So, with the slope aiding them, they seemed to have most things in their favour. But the mainspring of the team was Jean-Paul Dalechamps. He initiated every attacking move.

Mark realised it was time to take more positive action. When Kelmington ran the ball over the dead-ball line for a goal-kick he darted across for a word with Jerry Rendell.

'Look, I want the French guy marked out of this match – completely neutralised,' he told his team-mate.

'I want you to stick to him like super-glue, O.K.? Don't let him touch the ball if you can help it.'

'But I'm a striker!' Jerry protested. 'I'm no good at shadowing guys and putting 'em out of the game. I'm—'

'You're strong and you're fast and that's what I need at the moment to control their danger man,' Mark cut in. 'You're playing for the *team*, Jerry. If you shut Dalechamps up in a cell then it's as good as scoring a goal for us.'

Then Mark raced back to take up his own position in midfield before Rendell could voice any further objections. He was relying on Jerry to use his ruthless streak where necessary: but he could only hope that the winger wouldn't hurt his opponent or get sent-off.

When, a few moments later, Hedger's made a rare raid into enemy territory and almost reached the penalty area, it was Mark himself who thoughtlessly swung the ball out to the right wing. He'd expected Jerry to be coming up like an inter-city express to take the ball to the by-line and so pull Kelmington's defence apart. But Rendell was following orders and sticking close to Dalechamps in midfield. The ball rolled over the line for a throw-in to a grateful Kelmington defender. Even Justin Greene raised his eyebrows at Mark's incompetence.

Almost at once, Kelmington were slicing into their opponents' half again and Mark dropped back to assist his hard-pressed defence. He had the impression that several of his team-mates were already quite tired. Some of them, no doubt, had been late to bed the previous night – a Friday, of course – and that lack of sleep was affecting them. But nothing was taking a greater toll of their strength and stamina than the notorious slope. It really was hard work to keep propelling the ball uphill all the time and Mark kept thinking of the relief they'd all experience in the second half when it was their turn to sweep *downhill*.

Then, once more, the irrepressible Dalechamps sparked off another incisive attack from just inside his own half. He eluded Jerry Rendell, his shadow, simply by spinning round through 360 degrees and taking the ball with him. Jerry was left looking dazed, as Jean-Paul then whizzed forward and past two startled defenders.

Mark himself tried to cut the French boy off, but Jean-Paul's body swerve was too good for him. Without pause, or appearing even to look up, Dalechamps then sent the ball with his left foot into the middle. The tall striker and Perrett rose simultaneously – but it was the attacker who climbed the higher. His aim was every bit as good as his supplier's and the ball dropped into the net close to the angle of the crossbar and the near upright.

Bobby Storr had tried to punch the ball clear and missed it completely.

The goal-scorer stumbled as he landed because Perrett had fallen in front of him. Unavoidably, he crashed down on Perrett's arm and there was an audible crack that made Mark wince.

While the home fans deliriously celebrated the three-goal lead Mark Fox watched, aghast, as Kelmington's physiotherapist attended to the injured player. Ricky Perrett was white and perspiration was beading his face. He knew, and Mark Fox knew, that for him the game was over.

‘How do we come back from three goals down and the loss of our centre-back?’ Mark asked despairingly.

No one answered him.

Chapter Three

In the visitor’s dressing-room at half-time the despondency of the players was deeper than Mark Fox had experienced with any team. Few of them had ever seen such a bad injury to anyone and it had sickened them. Even Mark, who’d had a few scrapes of his own, both on and off the football pitch, hadn’t witnessed such a bad break. Now, to most of the players, the eventual result of the match mattered little. In any case, they would have said it was a foregone conclusion.

Mark knew it was his job to try and lift their spirits. Both sports masters had gone to the nearest hospital with Perrett and it was unlikely either would be back before the start of the second half. So there would be no encouragement, or shrewd words of advice, from Ted Bayley: but, Mark reflected, that wasn’t unusual. Quite possibly, Ted was thankful to be away from the scene of the disaster that had overtaken his team.

‘O.K., lads,’ Mark called, suddenly splintering the silence, ‘let’s stop moping and start thinking positively. O.K., so Ricky Perrett’s broken his arm – but that’s just one of the hazards of the game. But it’s not like – like a murder. People get over broken limbs. Bones heal and afterwards are as good as ever. So although we’re all sorry for Ricky there's no point in letting the injury flatten us all completely. We've got to go out of here for the second half in the right mood, believing we can still win this game.'

Mark paused, but no-one spoke. The players who were sucking oranges didn't even take the fruit from their lips. They still looked, in Mark's view, punch-drunk. He wondered how Buzz Burton, Athletic's youth coach, or even Albie Jones, his friend and former team-mate for several seasons, would have handled what was supposed to be a pep talk. How would they have aroused the interest and commitment of these players.?

'Look, I know most of you think we've had it just because we're three goals down,' he began again. 'But that's rubbish. Teams have come back from worse positions than this. And we've got plenty going in our favour. We'll be playing *down* the hill this half, not up it. Ben here has slotted brilliantly into Ricky's place in the back four. Kelmington are bound to be a bit sick about what they did to Ricky, you know. They'll play it cautiously, I reckon. Well, we can exploit that situation. We've already made plans to wrap up that French guy. Jerry's making a good job of looking after him – and he's the one who sparked off their goals.

'So, with a really determined attack, we can do it. When we win, it'll be a game they'll talk about – they'll remember – for years. And after beating this lot we don't have to fear anybody in the Cup.'

It wasn't, Mark himself realised, very inspiring stuff. It wasn't even true. Ben Cooper had been very shaky since coming on as a substitute for Ricky Perrett, almost as if he expected to suffer the same fate. And Jerry

Rendell had signally failed to keep a grip on Dalechamps. Still, by praising them publicly he hoped they would respond with improved displays.

'Anybody got any other ideas?' he asked with false cheerfulness. 'I mean, somebody could have seen something important happen out on the pitch that I missed. If it'll help, let's know about it.'

'I think one of their centre-backs – that big, blond-haired guy, you know the one, Mark – well, I think he's carrying an injury of some sort,' said Justin Greene rather hesitantly. 'He keeps holding his side as if he's in pain. Also, he's one-footed. He uses his left for everything. Really, he ought to be a left-back or somewhere like that.'

'Well done, Justin!' Mark responded enthusiastically. 'That's good thinking, *very* good. We'll play on that weakness.'

Justin would have been entitled to smirk. Instead, he just nodded soberly.

The half-time interval had been extended because of the serious injury to Perrett and that was why the players had been sent back to the dressing-room instead of remaining on the pitch. Now, as they returned down the lane to the playing field, Mark noted that most of them were looking a bit brighter. The longer interval was bound to have benefited Hedger's more than their opponents, who were so much on top in the first half.

Hedger's received some sympathetic cheers from spectators on taking up their positions but it wasn't long before all the support had shifted back to Kelmington, who resumed as if they meant to double their score.

Mark accepted that without surprise. There was no point in Kelmington sitting on their lead for the entire forty minutes of the half if they could add to it. Another goal for them would surely be enough to clinch victory: and that was what the home skipper had in mind. Not for the first time, Mark wished fervently that he'd chosen to play the other way on winning the toss. He'd made a tactical error, and was just thankful that Ted Bayley wasn't present to keep reminding him of it.

By dint of some good defensive collaboration by the back-four, in which Ben Cooper shone, and some touches of luck, Hedger's survived the opening assault. The striker who'd accidentally broken Perrett's arm hadn't allowed the incident to affect his attacking play: and Mark didn't blame him for that. In the circumstances, he would have hoped to do the same.

Then, after giving his defence some help, Mark at last saw the opening through which to launch a raid. It was generally recognised that his greatest assets were his electric initial pace and his close control of the ball. Now he used both to devastating effect.

Kelmington had at last over-committed themselves in attack. Their midfield had gone up in support of the attackers and so, when Mark intercepted a badly-struck pass from Dalechamps to a team-mate, the gap was wide. Instantly, he accelerated and was across the half-way line before an opponent could turn and give chase. Justin, who'd eagerly been awaiting an opportunity to take on defenders, raced up to give support. Behind them Brian Torson was also getting into top gear. With luck, it was going to be three-against-three.

With a dip of his left shoulder and a change of pace, Mark swept past his lone challenger. Justin was easily out-pacing his marker – if marker was the proper term in the circumstances – but Mark had no intention of passing to his team-mate. There was simply no need.

There was no alternative for the goalkeeper but to come out and try to fling himself at the ball as Mark raced towards the penalty area. He did so – then hesitated – backed up for a couple of metres – and finally dived at Mark's feet. Unfortunately for him, Mark had already switched the ball to his other foot, side-stepped, and was facing an empty net.

Quite unhurriedly, but firmly, Mark slid the ball home exactly midway between the posts.

Justin, of course, darted across to congratulate him but Mark treated the goal as no more than his due following such slip-shod defensive work by opponents. In any case, Hedger's needed to get another before they could consider themselves back in the game.

Five minutes later, with Kelmington beginning to settle down again after a rather jittery spell, Mark took the initiative again with a strong run from his own penalty area. He'd discovered, when scoring his goal, that he wasn't at all hampered by the degree of slope when running at speed downhill: his close control was as good as ever. Once more, he baffled opponents by feinting to go one way and shooting past them on the other side. Out of the corner of his eye he spotted Justin's presence – and at the right moment he gave his fellow striker the ball.

It was the sort of chance Justin had been praying for: and praying that when he got it, he wouldn't make a hash of it. As with Mark's run to goal, the path ahead of him was practically clear.

Justin surged away and the Kelmington defence hastily tried to re-assemble to cope with the threat. Naturally enough, they supposed that the chief threat was from Mark Fox, even though he'd passed the ball to someone else. Until he'd scored, Mark hadn't seemed to be half so dangereous as they'd been warned he was. His reputation, they'd decided at half-time, was inflated. Of course, they conceded, he had spent most of his time defending, but . . .

As he headed for goal without being threatened in any way Justin suddenly suffered a temporary loss of nerve. He was aware that Mark was moving on a parallel course and it occurred to him that the skipper was just waiting for a pass. It hadn't registered with Justin that Mark was being closely shadowed at the moment. Quite unnecessarily, Justin flicked the ball sideways to his co-striker.

Mark made no attempt to take possession of the ball – and he gave his marker no chance to tackle him. With the inside of his left foot he punched the ball several metres ahead of his team-mate and yelled: 'Go!'

Justin went. The one-two had distracted the defender in front of him – a full-back who'd sprinted across to provide cover, however flimsy – and for the second time the goalie was on his own.

As he picked up the ball Justin stumbled slightly – and that minor slip caused the goalkeeper to make a snap decision. He wouldn't came out. And that decision proved to be the wrong one.

For Justin instantly recovered his balance on the

incline and, advancing only another two paces, he swung powerfully with his right foot to crack the ball into the top corner of the net. The goalie was stranded, flat-footed.

'Well-done – but we still need more,' was Mark's reaction as he went across to praise the goal-scorer. There really was no point in getting excited yet. With the game in its last quarter Hedger's still required another goal to have a chance of staying in the Wrigley Cup competition.

Understandably, Kelmington were rattled. A three-goal lead had seemed to them to be invincible. Now there were hurried consultations in which Dalechamps was clearly the prime mover. Rather belatedly, the cover for Mark Fox was about to be reinforced. The defence was augmented by the tall striker. They would have liked some further direction from Barry Ridgefield, but he was still absent.

Kelmington's greatest asset in such a situation, however, was that they were used to defending against the slope. It was always their practice to attack in the first half if they were given the chance, and then hold the lead they almost invariably gained.

Mark, anticipating that he would come in for extra attention for the remainder of the match, had dropped back into midfield with the aim of taking the two players out of Kelmington's defence. He was still plotting to expose the right-foot weakness of their blond central defender. It had worked pretty well with Justin's goal because Justin had automatically cut inside the player he'd already summed up so well. It could work again.

'When you get the ball, go through the middle,' Mark instructed Brian Torson, who so far had seen precious little of the ball. 'Forget about the wing, we're not going that way.'

Brian nodded. Recently he'd felt rather neglected. When he first got into the side Brian had been taken up by Mark and they'd developed a fine understanding. But since Justin's arrival, Mark had tended to switch his attention to the newcomer. Now Brian wanted to prove that he could do things his own way – and be a match-winner at the same time. So he, for one, was delighted to see the return of Ted Bayley. The sports master was the person Brian most wanted to impress these days.

Ted meandered to the touchline and stood there. When someone told him the score he was surprised, but not heartened by the news that Hedger's were now only one goal down. He sensed that they wouldn't win. It was that sort of day. Ricky Perrett, the hospital said, should be all right because the break was a clean one, though complicated. But Bayley had moulded Perrett's style and given him great encouragement; he just hoped that this wouldn't affect his confidence and skill too badly. Ted felt so depressed that he couldn't even send out a message to his players. He remained on the touch-line, saying nothing, just moodily watching Hedger's on the attack.

The attacking ploys that Hedger's were using were not coming off now. Dalechamps, as if gifted with second sight, had re-organised the defence so that the one-footed defender was out on the flank after all. The tall striker had been slotted into a central position and was under orders to take care of Justin Greene.

Kelmington were at their most stubborn and succeeding in frustrating every raid. Mark's plan to play far behind his attackers was simply not coming off. Then, when he decided to go forward because time was running out, he chose precisely the moment when he could have helped the defence.

Suddenly, the ball was booted powerfully out of Kelmington's penalty area. Almost the entire Hedger's side was committed to attack and not one of them turned quickly enough to retrieve the ball. Then Kelmington's tiny left-winger, who had hardly been noticed throughout the match, sprinted forward with astonishing acceleration. It was almost as if he'd been waiting for 75 minutes for that split-second of action. Now, picking the ball up in his stride, he had only one opponent to contend with before reaching the box.

Ben Cooper hesitated, though not for long, before deciding what to do. He knew that he was the only one who could stop the little Kelmington player, and he went in like a scythe, determined to chop down whatever was in his path.

The winger stumbled as Ben's sweeping boot caught his shin: but he recovered instantly and flitted away again as Ben himself tumbled to the ground. Flapping his arms dramatically, the referee indicated that there should be no hold-up: he was playing the advantage rule. The winger kept his nerve as Bobby Storr rushed from his line and, very coolly, he slipped the ball beyond the goalie's reach and into the net by the near upright.

The home fans erupted and one or two even ventured on to the pitch to acclaim their new hero until members of the teaching staff ordered them off. Serious crowd disturbances could result in a school's team being ejected from the Cup competition.

For Hedger's, that fourth goal was the killer blow – and most of the players knew it. Mark had been aware that Hedger's were vulnerable to a swift breakaway because of the way the match was being played; but it was ironic that the break should come in just the precise moment that he himself had ventured into an attacking position. Still, he doubted that he'd have been able to cut off that fleet winger and no one could blame Ben for not halting the boy. The result had been determined in the first half when Kelmington had played superbly and used the slope to maximum effect in establishing that three-goal lead. If only Hedger's had known about the slope beforehand, and been able to anticipate Kelmington tactics, they might have been better prepared. At least, he reflected, they hadn't done too badly to pull two goals back.

So, when the final whistle sounded, Mark tried to look cheerful when he led the traditional three cheers for the victors in a schools' competition. He knew that although Kelmington deserved their win, Hedger's had acquitted themselves pretty well.

As the players left the field Mark caught Ted Bayley's eye, so he raised his eyebrows and give a grimace which was intended to say, 'Well, that was just the way it goes sometimes.' Ted, however, appeared deliberately to look away. Next moment he was answering the inquiries from some of the players anxious to know about Ricky Perrett's fate. Mark paused long enough to shake hands with Barry Ridgefield and receive his commiserations on their defeat.

'Hope you'll go on to win the Cup now we're out of it,' Mark told him. 'Then at least we'll have lost to the eventual winners.'

In the later stages of the match the weather had turned humid and most of the boys were glad to have the chance of a long and refreshing shower in the luxurious changing-rooms. Inevitably, there were various attempts to analyse the match and decide what had really gone wrong. No one, though, seemed to be blaming him for choosing to play against the formidable slope, Mark noted. Then Brian Torson remarked that the result didn't matter that much because there'd be another chance of winning the Wrigley Cup the following year. It was only then that Mark realised he'd probably played his last Cup fixture for Hedger's. In a few months he hoped to leave the school and sign for Athletic as a full-time apprentice. It was sad to finish on a losing note this season. But at least he'd played in one Cup Final for Hedger's, in a previous season, and also won a cap as an England junior player in a youth tournament played in Switzerland.

No one was in a great hurry to leave because, as promised, Kelmington had laid on a buffet meal for both teams.

The food proved to be every bit as good as predicted and Mark was tucking into chicken-and-ham *vol-au-vent* when Ted Bayley suddenly appeared at his side.

'So, you've failed *again*, I gather,' he remarked forcefully. 'How do you account for that, Fox?'

One or two of the other players in the group surrounding Mark were surprised by the fierceness of the sports master's expression; Mark tried to take the comment coolly.

'Oh, well, they're a pretty good side, you know,' he said. 'We can't win 'em all, can we?'

'I don't actually remember you winning *anything* for *us*,' Mr Bayley continued unrelentingly. 'For yourself, yes. For us, no. What would you say, Fox, was your contribution today?'

Mark hesitated. He sensed that Ted was on another of his witch hunts, and there was nothing Mark could do to head him off.

'Well, I did score a goal – and I think the other lads will agree I set up the one for Justin. But, well, overall—'

'Overall, you did *nothing* worthwhile as far as I could see,' Bayley cut in. 'You made the wrong decision when you won the toss, you let them take charge of the game and run up a winning score and then you hang about in the midst of our own defence doing absolutely *nothing*.'

'Oh, come on, sir, that's not fair!' Mark was stung. 'I was lying deep to draw their men out – pulling their defence out of position. We'd scored two and they were closing the game up and so it was a different way for us to attack.'

The sports master's laugh was as harsh as any of them had ever heard it.

'That's the best yet! I've heard that attack is the best form of defence – but never before has anybody tried to tell me that defence is the best way to attack! Not for the first time in my experience of you, Fox, you'd given up the ghost when we were losing. You were doing nothing because you were saving yourself for somebody else's game – your precious Athletic, no doubt.'

By now there wasn't a person listening to Ted Bayley's tirade who didn't look shocked. He appeared not to notice.

'Anyway, Mark Fox, I for one have had enough of your lack of loyalty to the school that's given you everything. I'm not going to have a captain who thinks only of himself. So, from this moment, you're relieved of the captaincy of Hedger's School team. And you're also suspended from *playing* for the team until further notice.'

Mark tried to swallow the piece of ham that was still in his mouth: and it almost choked him.

Chapter Four

Albie Jones was like an advertisement for good health. Where it wasn't actually glistening, because of the liniment and oils he had rubbed into it, his skin appeared to be glowing. To Mark's eyes, Albie's calf muscles appeared to have developed to the size of small melons and there seemed to be not a gramme of surplus flesh on his stocky frame.

His racing bike, now leaning casually against one muscular thigh as he stood at Mark's front door, was handsomely painted in light blue and scarlet. In its newness, it sparkled like its owner. Mark thought there wasn't much of it, but then he knew little enough about time trials and road racing on bicycles.

'You know what, Mark? You look washed out,' Albie

was saying in a more serious tone than he usually employed.

'Thanks very much – I like *you* too,' replied Mark coldly. 'If you'd had to suffer what I've had to suffer recently, you'd be looking washed out.'

'Well, then, I reckon I've dropped in at just the right moment,' Albie countered. He decided, for the moment, not to inquire into the cause of his friend's recent suffering. 'I thought you might keep me company while I test this new bike. Fresh air'll obviously do you a power of good tonight.'

'You expect me to run alongside you while you pedal like mad, is that it? No thanks, Albie, not on your life —'

'Look, mate, I know that *I* am crazy but I don't assume that everyone else is mad!' Albie cut in exasperatedly. 'I've still got the old bike, so you can ride that. I'll trust you not to knock it about.'

'Oh, and I suppose you just happened to bring it with you, hidden in your saddle-bag —'

Albie said crisply: 'Give it a rest, Mark. Whatever it is that's niggling you, a ride'll do you good. Just nip on your own bike and follow me to my place, right? Then you can switch to my old bike and we'll go for a sharpish ride round the industrial estate. That's where the next racing club meeting is to be held and I want to get familiar with the course. And I reckon you'll feel more comfortable if you put on some shorts, like me, or your track suit if you're ashamed to show your lily-white legs. Have you had your evening grub?'

'Yeah, we've eaten – nothing great but it filled up a hole.'

'Right, then, I'll try and be patient for the two

minutes dead it's going to take you to get ready, mate. By the way, how's your old lady? I always get on well with her and —.'

Suddenly, Albie's eyes opened wide as Mark's mother, as if on cue, appeared at Mark's shoulder to see who their visitor was. He guessed she must have heard his description of her. Mark somehow managed a grin and then departed upstairs.

'Oh, hello, Mrs Fox, I was just asking about you,' Albie said as breezily as possible.

'So, I gathered, Albie, so I gathered,' she replied with as straight a face as she could manage. 'Nice to see you again. How's the job going – the removals business you're in, isn't it?'

'Oh, great! Good for the muscles, you know – really gets you fit. Humping all that heavy stuff in and out of vans, up and down stairs, well, you've got to be fit to survive. The hours are good, too, because a job halfway across the country can be two days' work, non-stop, but then you get extra time off or extra money. Or both, if you're really in luck!'

'So that's how you can afford a new bike when you want one, is it? Mark's always saying —'

'Ah, but you see, Mrs Fox, there are other benefits to being in the removal business, if you're really on the ball. I mean, all sorts of deals you can set up for people who want to get rid of pieces of furniture they're fed up with, or pieces that won't fit into the new house they're going to. I've made a few contacts in the trade, so I know just where I can sell an item for the best price – with a bit of profit for me for handling it.'

'Oh yes, Albie! I remember your flair for setting up

profitable little business deals whenever the opportunity arises. And how's the football going? Which team is it you're with now?'

Albie fiddled with the handle-bars and the gears.

'Oh, er, I'm still playing for Watchford United – in the Zenith League, you know. But, well, they're having a bit of a thin time of it at the moment. We need somebody like Mark, you see, to gee us up a bit.'

'Well, I shouldn't think there's much chance of that, Albie,' said Eleanor Fox, sounding genuinely reluctant to have to admit it. 'As I'm sure you realise, the only team nowadays that Mark has any time at all for is Athletic. It's a pity really, because I've always thought you two got on particularly well together, even if I did worry dreadfully about what on earth you might get up to next, the pair of you!'

'Ah yes, those were the days,' agreed Albie, putting on his mock pensioner voice. 'Anyway, how's the writing coming along? Written any best-sellers lately?'

She laughed. One of the things she most liked about Albie was that he was never down-hearted for long. 'Er, no, not that I know of! Sold a few articles here and there – and even a short story, which isn't the easiest thing for a freelance writer to do. No, I can't even say I'm in the First Division yet, Albie. But I keep plugging away.

'Tell you one thing, Mrs Fox, I like your new hair-style. *Really* suits you.'

'Well, *thank* you, Albie! That's the nicest thing any young man has said to me for ages. Well, *any* man, come to that. Why, I'll bet that neither of my sons would even *notice* that I'd got a new hair-style.'

Mark, now attired in black shorts and a track-suit

top, brushed past his mother and went to collect his battered bike from the carport where his sister Karen had left it.

'Don't know what time I'll be back but I don't suppose I'll be late,' he announced as he manoeuvred his bike past Albie. Then, before he pedalled away, he glanced over his shoulder and tried not to grin. 'Oh, by the way, Mum, I like your new frizzy hair-style. Don't suppose anybody else does, but I do.'

Mrs Fox put her hands up in mock-surrender. 'It's a blooming conspiracy when you two get together,' she declared.

At Derby Road, where Albie lived, the switch of the bikes was made quickly – but not quickly enough to avoid an encounter with Mrs Jones, a fierce-eyed, bossy woman who always addressed her only son as Antony, which was his first name. It was Albie himself who'd chosen to use a shortened version of his second name, Albert. He regarded 'Antony' as far too soft for a powerfully-built future England international footballer and globally acclaimed club manager.

'You're not going out *again*, Antony, are you?' she called to him. 'I've told you a thousand times, you'll finish up with a broken head through riding that bicycle dressed in practically nothing.'

'Don't worry, Ma, we're just having a little spin on the estate and the roads'll be empty at this time. You know I can take care of myself.'

'Aye, just like that time you broke your ankle in that motor-car that turned over,' she muttered, plainly not convinced.

Albie waved and gently eased away from the house.

‘Why can’t she be like your mother, and just get on with her own life?’ he complained to Mark. ‘Never lets up, does she?’

‘Don’t know where you get the idea from that *my* mother doesn’t worry about things,’ Mark replied. ‘She’s always worried about illness and injuries. I reckon she thinks that every time I go out on to a soccer pitch I’ll end up with a broken leg at the very least. Actually, she’s never quite got over that bad knock that Barry got when he started with Athletic Reserves. She seems to think that lightning strikes in the same place twice. To be fair, though, she hasn’t mentioned it much lately – you know, since I actually started playing for Athletic.’

For a couple of miles they cycled together companionably and gradually Albie heard the story of Mark’s disastrous experience at Kelmington the previous Saturday. Mark was still furious at the humiliation of being banned from the Hedger’s School team, and was deeply worried about how the suspension might affect his standing with the staff at Athletic F.C.

‘I mean, I wouldn’t put it past Bayley to phone Gareth Blake, Athletic’s manager, and suggest that the suspension should extend to the club as well – I mean, that’d be typical of Bayley’s mean-minded attitude. He can be really vindictive when he’s in the mood.’ Mark frowned. ‘You see, Albie, the club have always stressed that school football comes first for an Associated Schoolboy player. So if the school – my school – claims that I’ve been suspended because I’m *not* putting them first, well, it’s obvious Athletic’ll back them up and say the ban applies with them as well.’

‘Not necessarily,’ Albie said, after pondering the point. ‘You said yourself that they know sports masters can be jealous of star players in their schools. So Athletic will know what sort of guy Bayley is and ignore his – his tantrums. ‘Another thing, Athletic have already told you they want to sign you up when you’re seventeen and that’s only a few weeks away. They’re not going to risk letting some other club come along and try to tempt you to sign for them. After all, they had to beat off other First Division outfits to get you on schoolboy forms, didn’t they? They’ve already played you in the Reserves a few times and you got rave reports for that match at Maine Road. So, no, they’ll want to keep you, mate – and they’re not going to change their policy just because some crummy sports master blows his top when his team loses in a Cup-tie.’

As he reflected on those words, Mark felt heartened by them. Albie was talking sense.

He turned his head and smiled at his former teammate. Not so long ago Albie had been a tearaway: even more impetuous than Mark. Suddenly, though, he appeared to be older and wiser than his years. It was an image Mark would never have guessed Albie could possess.

‘What about you, then, Albie? How’re things at Watchford? Been sinking a bit, lately, haven’t they?’

‘Yeah, ’fraid so, mate. Going down and getting worse. I’m absolutely wasted on them. No heart there, you see, as well as poor material.’

‘Well, you can always move on, Albie, can’t you? I mean, you’ve never been afraid to find another club.’

That was undeniable. A team-mate of theirs had

once commented that Albie Jones had had more clubs than the British Open Golf Champion – and it wasn't meant as a joke. Albie, though, thrived on change: it was almost his life-blood.

'Yeah, well that's really what I came to see you about, Mark. I mean, I reckon you might be able to help.'

'You what! I thought you just came round to be matey – a social call.'

Albie had the decency to look slightly mortified. 'Er, well, yes, *of course* I did. But I also thought it was the right time to get you to put in a word for me with Athletic. Honest, I'm in cracking form at present – never been better – and it'd be criminal to any club to waste the chance to get me on their books. And with your connexions with Athletic, well . . .'

'Albie, you can't really suppose they'd take *my* word for your undoubted talents! I don't have any influence there, anyway – maybe I won't even have any *connexions* there after —'

'Don't get me wrong, Mark!' his friend cut in hastily. 'I know a player's got to be *seen* in action by the club. All I'm asking is for you to mention my name to the manager or coach and say I'm worth a trial. That's all I'm asking: to be given a trial. Look, I know what you're going to say: that I could write and *ask*. So I could – and no doubt join the hundreds of others who do just that. But a personal *recommendation* is worth a million letters. If I fail in a trial, well, that's just too bad. But at least I'll have had a go. So all I want from you is the chance to get in in the first place.'

'Well, I don't know, Albie.'

'Mark, it's not *much* to ask! I mean, I've done things

for you, haven't I? Don't forget that I was the one who had the idea of going to the West Country when we played those games for Rowbay Sporting Club. If you'd never gone there then you'd never have met Terry Mercer and probably you'd never have got into the England Juniors side for that tournament.'

'Hey, hang on, Albie! You can't claim the credit for that. I got picked for England strictly on merit. That's the way *every* footballer succeeds – on merit. Just because Mercer managed the tour party doesn't mean he had anything to do with my selection in the first place. No, you're out of line on that one.'

'I was merely pointing out, Mark, that I had a hand in the chain of events that led you to a cap. That's all. I agree with everything else. A player has either got it or he hasn't. Well, that's all I want from you – an introduction to Athletic. That would be your hand in the chain of events.'

Mark couldn't help smiling.

'You think it will take you on the road to an England cap, do you? Athletic just being a stopping-off point along the way?'

'Could be, mate, could be! As I say, I'm playing better now than ever, so I can't see how Athletic can turn me down.'

Mark had known all along what his answer would be but he hadn't been able to resist the opportunity to bait Albie. So often, Mark himself had been the victim of Albie's extravagant sense of humour.

'All right, then, Albie, I'll do my best. I'll put in a word for you. But don't let me down, show 'em I'm a good judge. I value my reputation there, you know. Oh, and I'll tell you this: if it ever comes to the point where you are picked in my place in the First Division for Athletic, I'll murder you! I swear I will.'

'Right, Mark, that's a deal! And I won't squeal, either.'

'Now that's settled, what about this industrial estate we're supposed to be going to? We seem to be on the edge of nowhere already and if we go on much longer it'll be too dark to ride these bikes with no lights.'

'Great timing, Mark. I always knew you had it. Because, next turn on the left and we're there. Then we can get down to some serious business and get the old legs going like supercharged pistons.!'

To Mark's amusement, the turning led directly to a long straight thoroughfare that was actually called Turnfast Road. It was bordered by factory units and acres of warehouses surrounded by tall, wire fences or plain brick walls. There wasn't a house in sight and it seemed unlikely that there would be any traffic at that time of the evening. So it was easy to see why Albie had chosen it.

'Talking about timing, I see you've got a stop-watch on your handle-bars,' commented Mark as he tried to adjust the saddle on the bike he was using. 'When do you use that?'

'Oh, for speed bursts, usually. This game's all about timings, you see. You've got to be spot on. But I've also been checking on the difference it makes when I get lower over the handle-bars. Amazing how much difference a bit more of a crouch makes. But you see, wind resistance is the real enemy. That's what you're fighting all the time.'

‘Glad we’re not fighting any heavy traffic,’ said Mark. ‘On this bike I wouldn’t fancy meeting one of those huge artics. Knock you over as soon as look at you, they would. *If* they see you at all.’

‘Well, they can sometimes be a lot of help,’ Albie pointed out. ‘Overtaking trucks, you see, creates a sort of suction effect – and that makes it possible for the rider to get into a higher gear than you’d normally manage. But, of course, you’ve got to be an experienced rider like me to get the most out of that!’

‘Of *course*,’ said Mark solemnly.

Albie, who’d been making minute adjustments to his own machine, now did a few knees-bend and running on the spot exercises to add, as he put it, further tone to his muscles. Mark was already beginning to feel a bit weary after a taxing day at school and the ride from home to the industrial estate. He decided he wouldn’t be attempting many speed bursts whatever Albie tried to organise. Moreover, the large chain-wheel of the bike was somehow more tiring to drive.

‘Right, well just follow me,’ the racing cyclist invited. ‘I’ll try not to get too far ahead. O.K.?’

‘O.K. But just remember I’m supposed to be here to provide you with company, not competition.’

Albie just laughed at that and, as Mark knew he would, he powered away from the imaginary starting-line at a tremendous pace. Antony Albert Jones was not one to miss the chance of showing off, however small and familiar the audience. Mark followed as well as he was able, building his speed up gradually. Unlike his play on the football field, he’d never found it easy to get into top gear immediately on a bike.

Crouched at the lowest possible angle, Albie drove himself as hard as he could and he was well clear of his solitary pursuer as he swept round the first corner and into another long, straight road. A couple of hundred metres from that corner a saloon car was parked, half off the road, in the entrance to a timber yard. Albie went past it with no more than a metre to spare instead of giving it a wide berth. Casually he noted that there were two people in the vehicle; one of them was a girl, sitting in the driving seat.

Mark turned the corner as Albie overtook the car. The gap between the riders seemed to Mark to be widening in spite of his own efforts to put on speed. Now, Mark, too, crouched lower and pedalled harder.

He was exactly level with the stationary car when, without warning, the driver's door opened.

There was no time at all for Mark to swerve clear. His front wheel clipped the door. Mark was thrown from the bike and landed in the middle of the road on his right thigh.

Then, agonisingly, he slid across the width of the carriageway until his head collided with the kerb. The impact knocked him unconscious.

Chapter Five

It was the continuous blare of the car's horn that really alerted Albie to the fact that something was wrong. Glancing round, he saw that Mark's bike was lying in the middle of the road and that someone was running across to the far pavement.

Albie came round in a wide sweep by using a factory entrance and, his heart beginning to pound with anxiety he arrived at the scene of the accident as a man emerged from the car. It was he who'd been pressing on the horn button and his face was now whiter than the paintwork of his car.

'He's – he's been knocked out!' the girl who was bending over Mark was saying in a voice that suggested she was on the edge of panic. 'He just – just – fell off and finished up over there.'

Mark's eyes were closed and, to Albie, he appeared to be peacefully at sleep. Albie, trying not to look too closely at the blood oozing from Mark's right thigh and forearm, felt for his pulse. In the same movement, he leaned across to listen for the heart-beat.

'He's going to be all right, isn't he? Say he's going to be all right!' the girl demanded.

The beat sounded steady enough to Albie, though he had no real knowledge of what he should be hearing. He experienced an enormous sense of relief that Mark was alive. But he knew that any head injury was potentially serious and therefore Mark needed medical attention as soon as possible.

'It just happened in a flash, didn't it? I mean, one second he wasn't there, the next he was,' the girl went on. She had to convince herself it was a complete accident and not her fault. 'I only just started to open the door. I mean, I was going to go back to the passenger seat, you see. I mean . . .'

Albie wasn't really listening; and in any case, the girl

had edged away as if she didn't want any further involvement in the incident. He was trying desperately to remember what procedure should be adopted when someone received a head injury. The victim had to be given the chance to recover as quickly as possible.

That was it! Albie felt a surge of relief as he recalled that the injured player should be rolled over on to his front into what was known as 'the recovery position': not flat out, but with one leg drawn up and the head resting against the forearm. Albie was strong enough to manage that manoeuvre on his own but neither the girl nor her companion offered to help.

The man, however, had now advanced across the road and, while telling the girl to shut up, was trying to assess the extent of Mark's injuries from a distance of several metres. His expression alternated between alarm and anger.

'Look, son, you'd better ring for an ambulance and get the experts on the job,' he advised with fierce urgency. 'No good messing about here when we don't know how things really are.'

Albie glanced up. He'd been thinking the same. It might be quicker, though, if the man used his own car to take Mark to the hospital.

'There's a phone box on the corner up at the top of this road,' the man went on. 'Best if you nip up there on your bike and dial 999. It'll be fastest that way. We'll look after your mate while you're away. Go, on, son, don't waste any time.'

At that moment Mark uttered a strange sound that was almost, but not quite, like a moan. Albie hesitated no longer. He jumped to his feet and grabbed hold of his bike.

'Make sure he's comfortable – better put your coat over him to keep him warm,' he called as he rode away. He saw the man nod that he understood.

The phone kiosk was exactly where the man had said it was, standing in a recess in the fencing. When he picked up the receiver he suddenly remembered that he hadn't any money on him: he had a second or two of panic before he realised that no coins were needed for an emergency call. Firmly, he dialled 999 and a very calm voice asked him politely which service he wanted. After replying 'Ambulance!' he had to describe his whereabouts and was then told to wait at the scene until the ambulance arrived; it wouldn't, he was promised, be long.

Because of the location of the box, he hadn't been able to keep an eye on the scene of the accident while telephoning. Now, as he dashed for his bike again, he glanced down the road. To his utter amazement, he could see that Mark appeared to be on his own. No one was kneeling or standing beside him.

The car had gone.

Incredible as it seemed to Albie, the people who had caused the accident had completely abandoned the injured victim.

Mark was lying just as Albie had left him so the couple from the car hadn't covered him with anything. He seemed to Albie to have perhaps a shade more colour in his face, though that could have been wishful thinking on Albie's part. His breathing was steady enough and the abrasions on his arm and thigh had stopped bleeding. The wounds, though, looked to Albie as if they'd be painful before they healed.

‘Oh, come on, come on!’ he muttered fervently.

The ambulance arrived before any other vehicle passed along the road. The two men gave Mark a rapid examination and then prepared to lift him, covered now by a warm blanket, into the ambulance.

‘Is he going to be all right?’ Albie asked anxiously. ‘I mean, he *will* be all right soon won’t he?’

The men exchanged glances. ‘Should think so,’ said one cautiously. ‘We’ve seen worse, haven’t we, Jack?’ His mate nodded.

Albie didn’t find the remark very comforting. He didn’t want to let Mark out of his sight again until he knew what the official medical diagnosis was; he’d realised he would have to contact Mark’s mother and he didn’t want to alarm her unnecessarily. Rather to his surprise, the ambulancemen had no objection to his travelling with them. But they weren’t keen on the idea of taking the two bikes as well.

‘We’re not supposed to but, well, as long as you get ’em out of sight the moment we get to the Infirmary . . .’

Though checking Mark’s pulse and examining his eyes at regular intervals, the ambulance attendant chatted with Albie on the journey and explained the kind of treatment Mark would receive.

‘If he wakes up before they start cleaning those grazes they’ll probably have to give him an anaesthetic – they have to scrub bits of gravel and stuff out of the wounds and disinfect them. Otherwise he might be left with permanent scars, a bit like a tattoo. I expect he’s had an anti-tetanus injection sometime but he may get a booster, just to make sure.’

‘Will he have to stay in hospital?’

The man nodded. 'Expect so – just for tonight, maybe, for observation. Can't be too careful with head cases, you know.'

When they arrived at the hospital Mark was whisked away promptly and Albie busied himself finding a safe place by the car park for his two racing bikes. For some minutes he put off the task that shouldn't really have been delayed at all: ringing Mark's home to tell his parents what had happened. He supposed the hospital might do that for him but he knew it was his responsibility, as Mark's friend.

A girl in the almoner's office told him he could make a call without charge. Albie crossed his fingers and hoped that Mr Fox would answer. But it was Mark's mother who picked up the receiver. She was, Albie thought admiringly, remarkably calm in the way she absorbed the news.

'Right, Albie, I'll be there as fast as I can. My husband's away so I've got the car. We'll be able to take you home afterwards – with your bikes, of course. See you soon.'

He was amazed that, at such a time, she was able to think of his problem as well. He hadn't told her that Mark might have to stay overnight; after all, that was an unofficial forecast. Now, he hurried back to Casualty, praying that it was wrong.

The news there, however, was only mildly encouraging. Although Mark was conscious again he was now undergoing a series of tests and X-rays and it was still too soon to say whether he'd be detained for the night or even longer. The nurse who spoke to him gave Albie the impression that for some reason she didn't approve of him. It was only then that he realised he was still in his racing gear. So probably the nurse thought he was responsible for the accident that had befallen his friend; that if they hadn't been tearing madly along a public road this would never have happened.

Although she looked a little flustered when she arrived Eleanor Fox sounded as calm as she was on the phone. From the staff she learned little more than Albie had done about Mark's condition: but from him she now extracted the full story of the accident.

'You mean,' she asked incredulously, 'that these people simply *disappeared*, leaving Mark lying there in the road, all on his own?'

Albie nodded. 'I couldn't believe it myself, Mrs Fox. Obviously, they must have felt guilty and were afraid –'

'But I've never heard of anything so heartless, so *callous*! He could have – *died* – for all they cared, for all the care they took. Did you hear their names, Albie? I know they didn't tell you who they were but, well, you might have gleaned something from what they said.'

This time, miserably, he shook his head. 'I honestly don't think they used any names – he certainly didn't, anyway. Now I think about it, it was as if he were planning to make a run for it even while I was looking after Mark. The girl was about my age but the man was a lot older. I don't think he was her father, though. More like her boyfriend. Well, she was sitting in the driving seat so she must have been driving when they pulled up there, so –'

'– or about to drive off, Albie,' Mrs Fox put in.

'No, I don't think so. That's why she opened the door, you see, to get out and change places with the man. An *experienced* driver would have looked in the mirror first to see if anything was coming – I mean, I'd just gone past myself – but maybe she was a *learner*. I'm positive the car didn't have "L" plates on, though, because I'd have noticed as I overtook – cyclists always go well wide past learner-drivers, you know.' Albie paused for a moment.

'That could be why they panicked and just pushed off as fast as they could,' Albie concluded. 'If she shouldn't have been driving that car, and they'd caused an accident, they'd be in deep trouble. The guy worked it out pretty fast, though, to get rid of me while they zoomed away.'

'I suppose that could be it, Albie,' said Mrs Fox. 'I just can't get over such criminal behaviour, though. And it is criminal to leave an accident victim unattended in circumstances like that. Once I've seen Mark I'll get on to the police. I suppose you didn't get the number of their car?'

He sighed deeply. 'Sorry! Never occurred to me at the time because all I could think about was helping Mark. It was a big Ford, white and fairly new. But that's all I noticed.'

Mrs Fox squeezed his arm. 'Never mind, Albie, you've done remarkably well as it is. That might be something for the police to go on. If nothing else, that young girl will remember to check before she ever opens a car door again. I imagine that they'll steer clear of the industrial estate in future – they'll expect somebody to be looking out for them.'

'Just hope *I* catch up with 'em one day,' Albie muttered.

It was another forty minutes, during which Mrs Fox became increasingly restless, before a doctor emerged to tell them that Mark had been put to bed in one of the wards. The X-rays had revealed no severe damage, though there was extensive bruising and Mark was likely to suffer pain before his various bruises and grazes cleared up. To be on the safe side, he was to stay in the Infirmary overnight. All being well, his parents could take him home next day.

'May I see him now, doctor?'

'Oh yes, I think so. But don't expect to hold a conversation with him. He's very drowsy and it'll be best if he can get straight off to sleep again. So just for a minute, eh? Oh, but I think you'd better be on your own. I gather, young man, that you've been very helpful but tomorrow will be soon enough for you and Mark to discuss the, er, the gory details of your adventure.'

So Albie waited patiently while Mrs Fox went off to see her son: but, true to her promise to the doctor, she was back in five minutes. She looked, Albie decided, relieved: not exactly cheerful, but no longer worried.

'He doesn't seem so bad but, plainly, he's shaken up,' she reported. 'I told him how marvellous you have been, Albie, and I think he understands. Anyway, come on, let's get home and then the night will pass a lot quicker. I expect you could do with a hot drink, couldn't you?'

Albie nodded keenly.

Mark had no idea what time it was when he awoke. He knew at once that he was in a hospital ward, though he couldn't remember how he'd got there. His mouth felt as dry as sandpaper and just about as uncomfortable. Although his head seemed as if it were enclosed in an iron band he managed to turn it to the right. Dimly he could make out objects – shadows, really – beside the bed, presumably on top of a locker. But he couldn't make out a glass or a bottle or anything to drink. He needed a drink, desperately, but he daren't try to call out.

Someone, quite close by, was snoring. It was an odd sound, a sort of snort-and-whistle. In a way, it was quite an interesting combination. Mark found that he was listening carefully, awaiting the next snort, then a whistle. He wondered if anyone else was awake besides himself. The ward wasn't completely dark – there seemed to be a light in the far distance, though that might be the entrance – and perhaps soon a nurse would come round the beds. Then he could ask her for a drink.

He moved his legs — and immediately felt a sharp pain in his right thigh. Biting his lip to stifle a cry, he tentatively explored the source of the pain with his fingers. The area seemed to be sticky with a kind of grease or liniment: now his fingers carried the odour of an antiseptic.

That very slight movement had left an ache in his leg: and that worried him more than anything. He couldn't remember hurting himself there. His leg wasn't in plaster – he was sure of that – but clearly it was damaged in some way. Was it a *permanent* injury? As a footballer he'd naturally suffered plenty of knocks and kicks to knees, ankles and shins; the most painful of all had been a groin strain. When that was at its worst he'd feared he'd never play football again.

He'd had several narrow escapes in the past. The

previous October, he'd only just escaped serious injury when there had been a fire in the farmhouse flat where the Fox family were spending a weekend. But the publicity surrounding the rescue of his sister, Karen, had brought him to the attention of the management at Athletic F.C. and soon afterwards he'd signed the Associated Schoolboy forms for them.

Suddenly he became aware how quiet it was in the ward. The strange snorer had apparently stopped snoring. Mark, feeling in greater need than ever of a drink, wondered whether he should call out. If, that was, his dry mouth would allow him to make enough sound to be heard. He experimented, and managed no more than a croak. Oddly, that might have been the cause of setting off the snorer again. Almost immediately, the snort-and-whistle sounds were punctuating the silence.

For no clear reason, Mark recalled the incident in which the black dog had shot across the road in front of the bus taking the school team to Kelmington. Justin Greene had made his remark about black dogs being like black cats in bringing luck. Certainly it had brought *bad* luck for Hedger's and for Mark himself. His suspension from playing for the school had damaged more than his pride: somehow it had undermined his confidence in his own abilities. In training sessions since then he had felt quite out of touch and he was fearful of what he would be told the next time he turned up at Athletic's ground. Would the club say that the suspension imposed by the school should also apply to playing for Athletic?

He tried to lick his lips to ease the discomfort in his mouth: but now his tongue felt as big as a football. He began to think he would die soon if someone didn't give him a drink. Surely a nurse would have to tour the ward at regular intervals to ensure that the patients were all right?

Mark suddenly remembered the time he had visited this hospital in the company of his brother, Barry, and Jimmy Terndale, one of Athletic's brightest young stars and one of Mark's heroes. They'd spent the evening, chatting to young patients and cheering them up. Then, only a few months ago, Mark had actually played in the same team as Jimmy, striking up a fine partnership with him on his debut for Athletic Reserves. On that occasion Jimmy had been hoping to rediscover his old form after injury and so win back his place in the first team. Generously, he'd later told Mark that the way they'd worked together had made all the difference to his game. Since then, Jimmy had regained his First Division form and been scoring consistently. Mark wondered now whether he would ever again play in the same team as Jimmy Terndale – at any level. It seemed unlikely unless Jimmy suffered a complete loss of form and was banished to Athletic's *third* team, Melton United, who played in the Zenith League.

The Zenith League! That was where Albie played, for Watchford United. Albie, who had asked Mark to fix a trial game for him with Athletic. Albie had said he was in cracking form and felt that he deserved to play in a better class of football. Well, probably he was right. If he got his chance now he might go straight into Athletic's second team – and the place he could take if he played as a striker was Mark's. Give Albie the right sort of opening and he would score – in more senses than one. Mark found it a disturbing thought.

He tried to move to a more comfortable position in the bed but, again, his leg pained him. He could remember riding Albie's bike into the industrial estate – and Albie's burst of speed – but then: what? A blank: that was all. So what had he done to his leg?

'Are you awake, Mark?' someone was whispering. He managed to turn his head and could just make out that a nurse was bending over his bed.

'You've been tossing and turning like mad!' she told him in a gentle, friendly tone. 'Do you want a drink or anything?'

He managed to tell her that a drink was exactly what he needed. So she helped him to hold a glass of water to his lips while he sipped a little of it. Then she offered to make him a hot, milky drink if he'd like one. He said he would, and she went off to get it for him. Only when she'd gone did he remember that he'd meant to ask her what was wrong with his leg and why it itched so much. But he felt very, very tired.

By the time the nurse returned with the warm drink, he was asleep again.

Chapter Six

One week later Mark was convinced he was fit enough to resume football training. As he told his mother that morning, he was impatient to get into action again. However, it was no surprise to him that she totally disagreed. In the opinion of Mark and his sister, Karen, their mother had always been excessively cautious in matters concerning their health.

'It's done you the world of good to be off football for more than week,' she told him as she scrubbed at the keys of her typewriter with an old toothbrush. 'I'm sure you'll benefit even more by waiting another week or so before you start kicking a ball again. Remember what the doctor told you, Mark: the body heals in its own time, you can't rush it.'

'He also said that it *tells* you *itself* when it's ready to go to work again,' Mark fired back, leaping out of the armchair in which he'd been lounging. It was a long time since he'd felt so restless. That feeling alone told him he was well enough to test his muscles and reflexes in a game or a practice session. 'Well, my leg feels as good as ever, and the grazes won't take long to clear up completely.'

'Mark, you can't risk another bang on the head at this stage of your recovery,' she replied solemnly. 'You surely don't need me to tell you that. The football world's not going to come to an end just because you have to give it a miss for a few more days.'

Mark decided that his only form of defence was attack. 'Well, you can't deny that fresh air and exercise are good for everybody – *especially* for ex-patients,' he told her spiritedly. 'And that's just what I'm going to have. Right now! So cheers – I'm off.'

And without giving her time to make any reply, he darted from the room and out of the house.

He really had no idea where to head for when he reached the main road. A kick-about was what he'd had in mind but there wasn't much chance of that on a

Wednesday morning. Because he'd so rarely been away from school for more than a couple of days he'd almost forgotten what it was like to be on his own in a midweek morning in early spring. It crossed his mind that he ought to visit his grandfather, Ralph Blackshaw, who lived on the other side of town. Mr Blackshaw was a former professional footballer who'd played most of his career in the Third Division; now he was retired, and Mark visited him whenever he had time. This morning, though, he needed to *do* something rather than reminisce about ancient games.

Automatically, he hesitated at the bus-stop. It was from here that he caught the bus that took him to Athletic's training ground during the holidays or early evenings. A bus was coming at that moment and, instinctively, Mark waited for it. He might just as well go to the training ground as anywhere. Just because he was off school with a sick note didn't mean he wasn't allowed to *watch* a training session. There were people he could usefully talk to, if nothing else. Buzz Burton, the youth coach, would be around; and he might even bump into Gareth Blake, Athletic's distinguished manager. Although Athletic had little chance of the First Division title this season, and had been knocked out of the F.A. Cup in the Fifth Round by Ipswich Town, they were challenging for a place in Europe. 'That's our ambition and we've *got* to achieve it,' Mr Blake had told the *Argus*, the local evening paper, at the weekend. 'Top clubs like us pay top wages and so we need the sort of income that is earned by competing against the best sides in Europe. If we don't finish in the top six in the Division then I shall consider that this season has been little short of a disaster.'

As he settled himself into his seat for the ride into town Mark reflected on that comment and applied it to his own position. The season had been disappointing, if not exactly disastrous for him. He hadn't made a breakthrough into the first team at Athletic – though, admittedly, not many 16-year-olds would expect to do that anyway. His appearances in the Reserves had been fewer than he'd hoped because of school commitments. His recent suspension from the school team was a severe blow to his pride, even though Ted Bayley was notorious for his fickle temper.

The cycling accident, however, might have been disastrous. Mark thought how lucky he'd been that his injuries had not proved more serious. His thigh was healing pretty well, though there would probably be quite a scar left; but he hadn't had a single headache since leaving the Infirmary. One odd thing, though, was the way his mind was a blank about the seconds immediately before being knocked from his bike. He could remember attempting to pursue Albie, and noticing that a car was parked on the roadside ahead – but nothing more until he woke up in hospital.

Naturally, Albie had been to see him several times and was full of concern for Mark's progress. He kept saying that he felt responsible for the whole thing, though, as Mark told him, that was nonsense. Albie had, on request, given him the details of what had happened.

Eleanor Fox had phoned the police as soon as she'd got home that night, and told them the full details of the accident and how the couple had driven off leaving her son seriously injured. The duty officer had said that she was quite right to report it, since there was an injury to a person involved, but he didn't hold out much hope of tracing the car or its driver without a registration number to go on.

She was very surprised, therefore, when the same policeman rang back later that night. A girl had rung the police station from a call-box, apparently to report the accident – but in fact, her main concern had been to find out whether Mark was all right. She hadn't given her name, simply said she'd seen the accident happen; but after Mrs Fox's call, the duty officer was able to guess it was the girl in the car. 'I reckon it was a company car, he was a married man, and they didn't want anyone to know they'd been together,' the policeman commented, wryly, and unless the girl could be traced, it was unlikely that any charges could be brought against anyone.

Very thoughtfully, Albie had refrained from reminding Mark of his promise to put in a word for him with Athletic F.C. Mark, however, hadn't forgotten it. He hadn't forgotten, either, that during his night in hospital he'd imagined that Albie might take his place in Athletic's ranks if he didn't make a swift recovery. Well, that was still a possibility, he knew. So it was up to him to set about reviving his career with Athletic as quickly as possible.

He changed buses in the town centre with a new eagerness to get to his destination. His one regret now was that he hadn't thought to bring his boots with him. He supposed he should have got clearance from his doctor to head and kick a ball again but there had been no time for that. What they would say at Hedger's if they'd known he was about to return to the sports field he didn't dare think.

When, at last, he turned in at the gates of the training ground, the game in progress was not soccer but head tennis. Mark had played it only once before and without much enjoyment: he knew that heading a ball was not one of the strengths of his own game, though it was with a header that he'd scored his first goal for Athletic Reserves in his unforgettable debut match at Maine Road, the home of Manchester City.

A net had been placed across the centre circle at a height some way above what was normal for a game of tennis, and the match was being played by two teams of seven players per side. They were mixed sides, too, made up of both full-time professionals and apprentices, and Mark knew most of those taking part, either by sight or through playing in the same soccer team. As with most training games, it was being contested furiously, and the staff who were not playing were grouped round the 'court' and shouting either encouragement or derisory comments. The referee was the first team coach, Ricky Smith, a former Sunderland striker.

'Come on, come *on*, you can get lower than that, Jimmy lad,' he was telling Jimmy Terndale, who quite lamentably failed to stoop to prevent the ball touching the ground, registering a point for the opposition. 'You'd have done better than that if you'd been faced with an open net at Wembley in a Cup Final.'

'I'd've belted it in with my right foot and ripped the net from its anchorage,' Mark heard Jimmy mutter.

Mark made his way round the perimeter of the pitch,

not wanting to intrude in any way; he felt already that he was something of an interloper. Associated Schoolboys – even those on the verge of becoming club apprentices – rarely turned up at training sessions, and then usually only by invitation. He wasn't surprised to see Buzz Burton, Athletic's youth coach, talking intently to one of the apprentice professionals and apparently making a point about involvement. The boy was taking it all in, though plainly he was unhappy about something. Buzz, as Mark knew very well, could make some stinging criticisms when he felt they were deserved.

'Hi, son!' he called out cheerfully enough on catching sight of Mark. 'Been wondering how you were. Missed you last Saturday.'

'Oh,' said Mark, brightening. That was the best news he'd had in ages.

'Yeah, some idiot I won't name missed a couple of real chances that you would have scored without raising a sweat,' Buzz continued. 'So we only drew instead of winning. Anyway, what are you doing here on a Wednesday? Still off school, are you?'

'That's right,' Mark agreed. He didn't want to say too much.

'Everybody round here seems to be going down with the dreaded virus,' Buzz said. 'God knows where it's going to strike next. But that sounded like a nasty accident you had. How're you feeling now? O.K.? No ill effects, I hope.'

'Oh sure, couldn't be better!'

For the next few moments Burton continued to advise the apprentice about the way he should conduct himself during the course of a match. The boy's weakness, apparently, was that he quickly lost confidence after missing a few tackles and would in Buzz's opinion, 'vanish for the rest of the game. We might as well pull you off the park for all the good you are to us.' Buzz derived his nickname from the unlikely fact that he kept bees as a hobby; and he believed totally in the value of honey as a food and, as he put it, zest-giver. Mark hadn't much doubt that at some stage of the riot act he was reading to the apprentice he would mention that if the boy would only eat more honey he'd have more energy to put into his game.

Mark, not wanting to be accused later on by the sufferer of eavesdropping, concentrated on the novel tennis match. Jimmy Terndale wasn't the only one clearly not enjoy this form of training. It suited the taller players in a team because they were used to heading the ball frequently during a match. On the other hand, smaller (and sometimes, therefore, better balanced) players who operated in midfield should have gained the greater benefit from it. Yet, as Mark had discovered from playing in a number of teams over the years, there were always some players who simply didn't like heading a ball in any circumstances.

Such players could, of course, always argue tellingly that the name of the game was FOOT-ball and therefore heading should only be a last resort. This argument didn't, however, score with Buzz Burton. He maintained that *any* part of the player's anatomy should be used if it would help to get the ball into the net – legitimately. Moreover, for those who thought that constant heading was a bit of a risk to the cranium (and some did), he pointed out that the ball being used for such games was of the lightweight type; usually it was a volleyball which, because of its high bounce, required even swifter reactions on the part of the players.

With the score at 18-14 – the target was 20 points and only the side serving could score – the game was in its closing stages, and it seemed that the younger team would win. Although they weren't divided precisely, the teams were composed of established professionals one side of the net and reserves and apprentices on the other. In soccer training the first team squad very rarely lost, whether it was a five-a-side game or a full scale practice match, but here, it seemed to Mark, they were showing less than their customary determination.

Serving, as someone yelled, 'for the match!' was Craig Greenway, one of the fastest and most talented of the young players on Athletic's books. Mark had first met him when they'd played together for the Reserves at Manchester and he'd been greatly impressed by Craig's left-footed skills and sheer pace. He'd got the impression that Craig regarded him as something of a rival, even though Mark was the complete newcomer. What counted with Craig was that he'd heard Mark Fox being described as 'quicksilver' and that was a description he thought should apply only to himself.

Craig was as sturdily built as Mark – though not so tall – and now he headed the ball to the side of the makeshift court instead of putting it to someone standing closer to him. The ball was nodded back into the middle by one apprentice and back towards the baseline by another. The aim, of course, was to confuse the opposition so that they didn't know where the attack was finally to be launched. Craig knew. He bobbed up in the middle to meet the ball as it was being passed laterally: and, very cleverly, he steered it just over the net with a sinuous twist of his neck muscles. No opponent had a hope of intercepting it.

So the score was now 19-14.

'Got your gear with you, Mark?' Buzz asked suddenly.

Mark was concentrating on the game so that at first it didn't register with him that the youth coach was addressing him.

'Oh, er no, sorry. I, er –'

'No matter, son. There's some spare stuff in the changing-room – plenty, in fact, with all these absentees. It's in the big wicker basket. So go and get yourself kitted out and Ricky'll slot you into the next game. Go on, son, don't hang about.'

Mark hastened over to the changing-room, but now that there was a chance of some action, he was almost reluctant to take it. He deliberated over choices of shorts and shirt when he got there. There was an attendant on duty – Athletic never skimped on providing proper staff and facilities – but he was busy with tasks of his own and didn't offer any advice apart from telling Mark to help himself. The players were wearing rubber-soled training shoes and there was an abundance of spare pairs.

Just as Mark was deciding that the third pair he'd tried on was the right one, Jimmy Terndale came in. The first team striker stood in the middle of the room in an apparent daze, as if trying to work out what to do next. Then he stumbled over to a bench and slumped with his back against the wall.

'Jimmy, are you all right?' Mark asked anxiously.

'Dreadful! That's what I feel, dreadful,' Jimmy replied in an appropriately doom-laden voice. 'The truth is, Mark, I feel like death.'

The very fact that he hadn't addressed him as Brother Mark – a favourite and friendly reference to the days when Jimmy had been a team-mate of Mark's brother Barry – was a clear indication that Jimmy wasn't exaggerating. Normally, he was the most cheerful and optimistic of players.

'Anything I can do to help!'

'You can't cure a throat that feels like a box of knives, can you? Or legs that weigh ten tons and ache from top to bottom? Look, I can't even see straight.'

In fact, he had his eyes closed. His face was grey. Mark felt at a loss. He fiddled with the training shoes and knew he ought to hurry up and get back to the tennis game. Buzz would otherwise want an explanation of what had kept him.

'Get yourself out there, Mark,' Jimmy said in an exhausted voice. 'But for God's sake don't tell Ricky Smith what I've told you. I don't want him to know I'm bad. He'd send me packing to bed and I'd have no chance of making the Liverpool game. I can't afford to miss that one. I've been out of the side already this season and it was the devil's own job to get back in again.'

'Sure, Jimmy. But, well, doesn't he *suspect* you're not feeling so good? I mean, he's used to seeing players with various knocks and sprains and other sorts of complaints . . .'

Jimmy opened his eyes briefly. 'That's not the same as *knowing*, though, it it?' he pointed out.

'Well, hope you're soon feeling better, Jimmy,' Mark said as he departed. 'They're going to need your goals against Liverpool. See you.'

As he'd anticipated, Buzz Burton asked what had kept him and Mark murmured something about finding shoes that fitted comfortably. Buzz, even though he wasn't in charge of the tennis, was looking harassed and curtly he told Mark to be ready to join in the game as soon as Ricky Smith gave the signal. In Mark's absence a new game had been launched and three points scored – all to one side. Some of the players had been changed round, others replaced and one or two were standing by for a call-up.

'Right, son, on you go,' Ricky suddenly told Mark. 'You're big and strong so you can operate near the base-line. So I want to see a lot of power put into your headers. O.K.?'

Minutes later Mark had to come to terms with the effects of his accident. The second time he headed the ball in the match, he felt a twinge of pain. It seemed to be located close to the scalp but he couldn't be sure just where it was. The ball, though, had gone just where he'd directed it. He hoped no one would notice his discomfort.

Mark bit his lip, hard. If the pain persisted then he'd just have to tolerate it. He wasn't going to miss the chance of showing Athletic's top coaches what he could do. So he threw himself into the game with gusto. He hungered for the ball to such an extent that at one point he even collided heavily with a team-mate because he didn't think to draw back. He hauled the player to his feet, apologising profusely.

'Don't go clobbering our own guys, Mark!' Ricky Smith called to him. 'We're down to minimum strength as it is. So we can't afford to lose players in *good* health . . .'

Mark managed a lop-sided grin at that. But it astonished him that Ricky Smith even knew his name. After all, Smith was the first team coach and could hardly be expected to know much about the associated schoolboys on the club's books. In the normal run of things, Smith wouldn't meet them at that stage of their development. So, fairly obviously, he'd learned Mark's name from Buzz – and remembered it.

The next time he tried a strong header Mark again experienced a flick of pain, but it was no worse than the first one. He could, he knew, cope with that. In any case, the light ball was unlikely to cause him any real harm. There had been no accompanying dizziness or any other worrying sensation.

For the next few minutes Mark seemed to be everywhere on the court: ducking, stooping, soaring, twisting to head the ball from all angles. His own exuberance was infectious and his team was completely in command of the set. Very quickly, they established a lead of 12-2. Ricky Smith, shouting encouragement and advice in equal measures, was delighted by such a show of enthusiasm. It was one of the rare bright spots of the week.

When the set was over Smith called Mark to him for a few words. First, he pointed to the scars on his thigh and wanted to know what had caused them.

'Er, fell off a bike,' Mark admitted shame-facedly. It seemed to him then the most stupid thing he'd ever done.

'Nasty things, bikes,' said Smith. 'Don't believe in two wheels, myself. Hurt, did it?'

'Well, at the time. But I've got over it. It was over a week ago.'

Ricky raised his eyebrows. 'Recent as that, was it? Well, good for you, son. Reckon you showed a lot of spirit today in everything you did. Keep it up. O.K., off you go now with the apprentices. Buzz wants to put you all through a bit of sharp ball work.'

Although Ricky Smith had dismissed the youngster from his presence, that wasn't the end of his interest in him. For the remainder of the session he didn't once take his eyes off Mark Fox.

Chapter Seven

Mark Fox stood and watched in astonishment as Ted Bayley, track-suited and sweating, burst through a narrow gap in a defensive line, while clutching a rugby ball to his chest in traditional wing-three-quarter style. In fact, he wasn't in any danger of being stopped in his tracks, of being hauled down in a strong tackle by a bigger or more subtle opponent: because the 'opposition' consisted of some of the youngest pupils of Hedger's School. None of them was going to risk the full ire of the sports master by attempting to stop him from showing off.

Hedger's had never been a rugby-playing school and so Mark couldn't imagine why Ted was suddenly demonstrating the arts of that game to the youngest boys. Had there been a dramatic change of policy with regard to sport since the school's defeat in the Wrigley Cup at Kelmington? Were Hedger's now intending to take up rugby in a desperate effort to win at *something*? That hardly seemed likely because the soccer pitches were still in existence and properly marked out. What's more, no rumours had been floating about on the subject of sporting changes. Still, there had to be some explanation for this mysterious coaching session that Mark, who'd been on his way home after his first day back at school, was witnessing.

Bayley now lobbed the ball to the thin-legged, dark-haired boy who had displayed so much promise in Mark's own coaching session of soccer. His name, Mark recalled, was Karl Jenson — and Karl was being told to demonstrate his ability to burst through a defence and reach the try-line.

Karl, however, didn't have the weight or the physical strength to bulldoze his way through the opposition, and was quickly pulled down. Two or three boys fell heavily on him and Karl was plainly winded. Mr Bayley brusquely told him to pull himself together and then turned his attentions to a group which had been formed to practise passing on the run.

As Karl gradually got his breath back Mark strolled towards him, determined to discover what was going on. Ted was so busy throwing the ball about and yelling orders that he wasn't aware of Mark's presence on the perimeter of the training area.

'What's all this about, then, Karl?' he inquired.

The boy couldn't disguise his pleasure when he saw

who was asking the question.

'No idea, but it seems crazy to me,' he replied, with the slightly nervous honesty of the first former. 'He just said we'd have a change this week from soccer. He said we needed to sharpen up and put more effort – more *beef* he said – into our game. Anyway, he rolled up with this rugby ball and that's what we've been playing – well, *learning* about, I suppose. Can't see what good it's going to do. It won't improve *my* soccer. Are you going to take over again, Mark?'

All Mark could do in answer to that question was to shrug his shoulders. Ted Bayley was obviously as unpredictable as ever.

'Er, I was wondering, Mark, if you'd had a chance yet to fix anything up for me at Athletic?' Karl now inquired tentatively. 'You know you said you might be able to arrange for me to look round the dressing-rooms and so on.'

'Oh!' Mark had completely forgotten about Karl's request. 'Well, the truth is, Karl, I haven't got round to it yet. I've been off school with this injury and I haven't seen much of the guys at Athletic. Tell you what, though: I'll definitely ask about it this coming Saturday. I'm pretty sure there'll be no difficulty in getting a visit fixed up for you. O.K.?'

'Sure, Mark. Thanks very much.'

The boy appeared so pleased that something would be arranged for him that Mark felt thoroughly guilty. But just then, Ted Bayley caught sight of him and signalled that he wanted to talk to him. Mark ambled across to where the sports master had taken up his position to watch kicking techniques being demonstrated by pairs of makeshift full-backs.

'Hello, Mark, nice to see you back,' Bayley greeted him with an enthusiasm and cheerfulness that surprised Mark. 'Recovered from that crack on the head, have you?'

'Oh, sure, thanks.'

'Good, good! Can't do with any more of our players being side-lined. It was bad enough losing Ricky Perrett with a broken arm.'

'How is Ricky?'

'Well, he's out for the season with an injury like that. But he seems cheerful enough, and I expect he'll be as good as new when he gets the plaster off. Anyway, it's good for all round morale to see you looking fit again. Gives us all new confidence for the future!'

Mark didn't quite know what to say. Ted Bayley had always been a man of contrasting moods, but Mark couldn't remember seeing him in such an exuberant state as this for a long time. He was talking to Mark like a long lost friend, yet, only recently, he had relieved Mark of the football captaincy and treated him with derision.

'Good kick, that, Gareth!' the sports master yelled to a slightly-built fair-haired boy who had punted the ball over the imaginary halfway line. Then he swung back towards Mark. 'Lot to be said for a bit of rugby training, you know. Instils a bit of real aggression and proper determination into a lad, don't you think? Good for all games, not just rugby. I reckon you should try it when you take over the soccer coaching again, Mark. Next week, perhaps, eh?'

'I thought I was supposed to be banned from anything to do with soccer at this school,' Mark said.

Ted Bayley produced a very fine imitation of a spontaneous, merry laugh.

'Oh, you don't want to take everything so seriously, Mark! We can't abandon our best player like that, can we?'

'I thought you had,' Mark muttered. He had the feeling that, somehow, he was being out-manoeuvred in some strategic game Bayley was playing.

'Oh, I was just a bit put out at the way we were defeated at Kelmington – bit of a shock, you know, a blow to the old pride,' the teacher rattled on. 'Must admit I'd hoped to go out on a high note, a *winning* note. But, well –'

'Go *out*?' Mark queried, genuinely puzzled. 'I mean, how can you *lose* on a *winning* note? Doesn't make sense.'

'Ah, that's because you're misunderstanding what I'm getting at, Mark,' was the smooth reply. 'I'm talking about *myself*, not Hedger's soccer team.'

Mark was still baffled.

The sports master sighed theatrically. 'O.K., I see I'll have to spell it out for you, young Foxy. I AM LEAVING. I-have-got-a-new-post-in-another-school. Get it now? Yes, I can see it's sunk in at last. I just credited you with a bit more intuition, that's all. The sort you display on the football pitch when you're on top form as a striker and sniff out an opening. Still, as I was saying. I'm leaving Hedger's at the end of the term to become head of the P.E. Department at a school just outside London. I thought it might have been nice to depart knowing that the team I coached – managed, if you like – had just won a trophy. So when you got knocked out of the Wrigley Cup, well, I felt a bit put out. In the end, though, what does it matter? That's what I ask myself. And the answer I always get is – not a sausage!'

'You —' Mark stopped himself just in time from giving vent to his anger as he realised the implications of Bayley's words. His own reputation with Athletic and future career as a footballer might have been ruined by the sports master's selfish, vindictive action after the Kilmington match. And it had not even been out of concern for Hedger's, but simply because of this job. Finally, he said, 'A much bigger school, is it.'

Ted beamed.

'Oh, *much* bigger. Much more scope.'

'And they play *rugby* there, right?'

'Right.'

'So *that's* the reason for the sudden switch to rugby training instead of soccer. I might, er, well – I –'

'Go on, Mark, say it: you might have *guessed*. Well, good for you. Shows your intuition's coming back. Just like you're coming back to take the soccer coaching now you're fully recovered from your little accident.'

'Pardon?'

At that moment the rugby ball, thumped too extravagantly by Gareth, floated down above them. Mr Bayley nonchalantly reached up to field it, and took it cleanly. He tucked it under his arm.

'Right, lads,' he yelled, 'that's it for today. You've had enough even if I haven't! For the time being, we're going to alternate the rugby with the soccer in the special training sessions. So, next week, it's soccer's turn. And the coach, once again, will be Mark Fox!'

Mark had sensed what was coming – and he wanted

to explode. This time, he really had been out-witted by the sports master because they both knew Mark would look very foolish, and immature, if he tried to turn the job down in front of the wide-eyed first formers.

The sports master was plainly expecting Mark to make some comment about how pleased he was to be re-instated. But Mark wasn't going to oblige him. Instead, he stalked away without saying another word.

It turned out to be a day of surprises and encounters for Mark. By the time he arrived home at the end of the afternoon he'd calmed down about Ted Bayley's conduct. He supposed that, after all, he might be doing something useful for the school if he encouraged some of the first year boys to develop their soccer skills. In a way, too, it would be good to end his school days on a relatively happy note. He wanted them to end, also, with a victory. So he was determined Hedger's first team would win its next match by a handsome margin. That would go a long way towards erasing all the unhappy memories of that disaster at Kelmington.

Because he had a lot on his mind, Mark failed to notice the bike propped against the garage wall. Therefore the subsequent sight of Albie lounging in an easy chair in the sitting-room was a surprise.

'Good to see you, mate,' Albie greeted him warmly. 'You look great! The old rest must have done you good. Knew it would! That's why I hauled you off to hospital.'

'Thanks a million,' Mark replied coolly. 'I suppose you've just dropped in to see if I want to buy a second-hand racing bike. Well, the answer's no thanks – not in a million years.'

Albie gave him an appraising glance as Mark

perched on the arm of a chair. 'You come into money, or something, the way you keep mentioning millions?'

'Nope. You're the one greedy for money. All I'm interested in is my football career. Anyway, what are you doing here apart from damaging the shape of that rather smart chair Mum bought last week out of her latest literary success?'

'Funny you should say that, old mate, because the devastating Mrs Fox was the one who *invited* me to try out this smart chair, as you call it. While, I should add, she herself is this minute fetching me a slice of her latest cooking success – a chocolate cake I think she called it. Oh, and a cup of coffee as well.'

'Feeding your face again at our expense! Look –'

'Hang on, hang on! You asked me a question, remember? Well, I was just about to answer it. What do I want, you said. Well, what I want, Mark old mate, is to know if you've done anything to further *my* career, as you promised. In other words, when are you going to tell me that you've fixed it for me to have that trial at Athletic? I mean, this is the right time for it. None better. With Athletic players dropping down with this virus by the minute – or so I hear. They must be desperate for good players like me – could even be *praying* for a guy with my sort of talent up front.'

'Er, yeah,' Mark said cautiously. Suddenly, it seemed to Mark that everybody was demanding something of him: Karl Jenson, Ted Bayley, now Albie.

'Well?' Albie said, impatiently. 'Don't tell me you've *forgotten*! I mean, you couldn't be as rotten as that, could you, Mark? To let a pal down with a thumping great crash?'

'Well, I've really had a lot on my mind . . .' Mark was beginning to say, when his mother came in with the promised cake and coffee. Her arrival saved him from having to invent complicated excuses. He smiled winningly. 'Oh, great, Mum! Is there some of that for me? No, don't go – I'll get it myself.'

'Goodness, he must be feeling energetic again,' Eleanor Fox remarked, as her son darted towards the kitchen.

Mark spooned coffee and one helping of sugar into a mug and, while he waited for the kettle to boil again, cut himself a generous slice of the chocolate cake after scooping up all the loose crumbs. It occurred to him that perhaps he was being a bit self-centred in not trying to give Albie – and Karl – the assistance they wanted. After all, it would cost him nothing in effort or time. Albie *was* a good friend – just about his oldest friend.

As he poured hot water on to the coffee and topped up with milk he promised himself that this coming weekend he would make a point of setting things up at Athletic for Karl and Albie.

Mark was just passing through the hall on his way back to the sitting-room when the phone rang. Automatically he put down his coffee and picked up the receiver.

'May I speak to Mark, please. This is Gareth Blake at Athletic.'

Mark couldn't suppress a gasp. The Manager telephoning him *personally*. Somehow he managed to say that it was Mark who was answering.

'Ah good, I thought it was. Listen, son, can you get down here to the ground in the next hour? There's something rather important I want to talk to you about. In person, that is, not over the phone. O.K.?'

Chapter Eight

By the middle of the following Saturday morning Mark was still finding it difficult to grasp all the implications of the news Gareth Blake had given him in the manager's office at Leeside Park. After all that had happened to him recently at school and at home it was hard to believe that, in less than four hours, he would take his place on the substitute's bench for Athletic F.C. in their home game with Liverpool.

Yet the twelve names that included his own had been listed in the local evening paper, the *Argus*, and he had been telephoned for his own comments by a member of the sports staff. Mark, who hadn't expected the call, was on the point of telling the reporter everything he wanted to know when his father whispered that it might be better to say little until he knew that Mr Blake had no objection. Most managers permitted their players to talk to the press but only on non-controversial matters. The reporter himself, however, said he'd already cleared the interview with the manager – and, in fact, it was Mr Blake who'd give him Mark's telephone number. So, in the end, Mark's reaction to his selection as a member of Athletic's first-team squad duly appeared in the paper. When he read it he was pleased to see that he'd been quoted perfectly accurately.

'I'm very flattered to be picked for this match, or any match,' said sixteen-year-old Mark (the report read). 'I'm also a bit amazed! I didn't think my chance would come for a long time yet. I'll just try and make the most of it if I get on the pitch.'

Mark didn't want to admit it, but he thought his chance of getting into the match was exceedingly remote. He was there to provide cover for any player who might be injured: he wasn't on the bench as part of a tactical ploy. Gareth Blake had told him as much and Mark was grateful that the manager had been so open and direct about his selection for the squad.

'There are two reasons for naming you as the substitute for this match, Mark,' Mr Blake had told him on that Thursday evening interview in his office. 'The first is that, as you know, we've had a terrible time with injuries and the effects of this virus that seems to be spreading everywhere. Every time the phone rings I expect it to be another medical report on another player who's gone sick. So I'm short of players and therefore I've got to make use of whoever's available. But the second reason is the more important one, Mark. It's this: that I think you're good enough to turn out for Athletic in a top match. If I didn't think that, I wouldn't risk you, make no mistake about that. We've got vital First Division points at stake and we want to get into Europe. But you've proved to me, in matches for the Reserves, and you've proved to Ricky Smith and Buzz Burton in training sessions, that you've got a lot of ability – and you've got a lot of guts. I need players like that, players who'll give me – and the club – everything when the going is tough. Believe me, Mark, the going *is* tough at present. But we'll survive.'

He paused at that point as if to give Mark an opportunity to say something if he wanted to; but Mark was finding it hard to listen with total attention to everything being said to him. His mind seemed to be whirling in all directions.

'I'm not putting you on from the start,' the manager had resumed, 'because I reckon that would be asking just too much of a lad of your age with no previous first-team experience. Especially against a non-stop running side like Liverpool. They never allow the opposition to settle down if they can help it, so you'd be under pressure every one of the ninety minutes. And that would be unreasonable, in my opinion. Having said that, though,' Blake continued, 'I also believe that a youngster loses nothing in confidence if he starts at the top — unless, of course, he's not good enough to be there in the first place. And that doesn't apply in your case, Mark. We have great hopes for you, son, and I have no doubt that you'll prove the truth of what I'm saying in the short term, not the long term. Now, is there anything you want to talk about to me, anything you want to ask?'

Mark shook his head. He still felt a bit dazed and he couldn't think of a single question.

'I'd just like to say, well, thanks, Mr Blake. I mean, I think it's fantastic that you want me to play for Athletic against Liverpool. But –'

Gareth Blake held up his hand as if to halt Mark's faltering comments. 'O.K., son, that's how it should be. Let the whole idea sink in and *then* decide if there's anything you want to ask about. Just absorb the good news. Then we'll have another chat on Saturday before the match. By then, you'll have got used to being in the squad. There'll be some publicity about your selection but we can handle that all right. I remember how well you coped in the direction when the papers got on to you after you'd rescued your sister from that fire. So you'll certainly be able to cope with this situation.'

His family, when he broke the news to them on arriving home that evening, rather surprised him by the warmth of their reaction. Karen, rarely demonstrative in anything to do with her brothers' interests actually kissed him quite enthusiastically and exclaimed that she hoped he'd hit a hat-trick. He tried to explain that probably he wouldn't be on the pitch long enough to score one goal, let alone three; indeed, he might not even get on to the pitch at all.

Hedley Fox seemed to agree with him on that point. 'I imagine, Mark, that the manager is really putting you on the sub's bench for the experience – to give you the ideal opportunity of soaking up the big match atmosphere. But, naturally, I hope I'm wrong. I'll be the proudest chap in the stadium if you get on to play against Liverpool. Liverpool – of all teams! What a start that'd be.'

Mark's mother was excited too, though she added a note of caution. 'What a wonderful chance! But are you absolutely sure, Mark, that you feel fit enough? I want things to go well for you, just as your Dad does, but –'

'Look, Mum, *of course* I'm all right. I told you before. I felt great after that training session. No trouble at all. Don't know when I felt fitter, to tell you the truth.'

He paused, and then added, 'Anyway, the club physio is bound to give me a check-up before the match. That's automatic. Athletic wouldn't play anyone at all who wasn't fit, especially in such a top match.'

'That's true, Eleanor,' her husband confirmed. 'These days the clubs seem to worry more about physical fitness than even you do! No, you can be sure they'd only let Mark on to the pitch if he was A1.'

Almost from the moment the news appeared in the evening paper the telephone began to ring at the Fox home with friends of the family wanting to offer their congratulations. Among them was Ted Bayley, who was still in a very generous mood and talked of the honour for Hedger's: rather more diffidently, he inquired whether Mark might have a spare ticket for the match. Mark, who'd been promised four by Gareth Blake, conceded one of them to the sports master before he could think of a good enough reason for refusing it.

Mr and Mrs Fox were, of course, going to use two of the tickets, and the fourth was reserved for Mark's grandfather, Ralph Blackshaw, himself a former professional soccer player. Over the years no one had given Mark more encouragement, or fired his sporting imagination more often, than his grandfather. Nowadays Mr Blackshaw rarely went to a League match, but he had long ago given his promise that he would attend Mark's first game in the First Division. So, not surprisingly, the silver-haired and very smartly attired Mr Blackshaw turned up in good time on Saturday morning for what he described as 'an early lunch and an afternoon of rare excitement – history in the making, you might say!'

For Ralph Blackshaw had no doubt at all that his favourite grandson would make his First Division debut in the game with Liverpool.

'And you must capitalise on it, young Mark,' Mr Blackshaw insisted. 'You must seize your chance and make the most of it, just as I did when I played my first match in the first team. Let them all see just what you're capable of, and then your career will be well and truly launched.'

'I'll do my best, Grandad, you know that. But, honestly, I don't think I'll get on to the pitch. You never know, by the time I report to the ground the Boss could well have had second thoughts and given somebody else the substitute's job. I mean, one of the players who's been ill could have made a miraculous recovery!'

'Mark, I don't think Mr Blake is the sort of chap to play tricks like that on a young player,' Ralph Blackshaw replied solemnly. 'I'm sure he's straight as a die and that when he says a thing, he means it. So you can take it from me that you will be twelfth man.'

At an appropriate moment, Mark escaped from the sitting-room and all the talk and speculation. He felt an overpowering need to be on his own for a time before he made his way to Leeside Park to join the rest of the players.

Whatever anyone else thought, Mark believed that he would only get into the game if there was an emergency such as a serious injury to one of the Athletic players. It really wasn't credible that the Boss would simply give him a taste of the action just for the sake of it: not in an important First Division match against opposition such as Liverpool, so recently holders of the European Cup and one of the most feared sides in world football.

On the other hand, if he did get on to the park, how would he acquit himself in front of probably the biggest crowd of his career? Normally, he didn't suffer from nerves, even on big occasions. All he thought about was getting possession of the ball and going for goal: he was a striker and so it was his primary job to put the ball in the back of the net.

As if to remind himself of past triumphs Mark got out his scrapbook of cuttings and began to browse through it. Then, as he turned a page, a letter slipped out. He knew at once what it contained: a formal invitation from the Football Association to play for England Juniors in a tournament in Switzerland. Instantly he recalled his first match on that tour – more than a season ago. It had been against Holland and on that occasion, too, he'd been picked as the sub. Then, when he'd been sent on to replace the injured England captain, he'd scored an own goal!

Hastily, he closed the book and slipped it back into the drawer. But that dreadful experience in Switzerland stayed in his mind. All he could hope was that it wasn't an omen.

Chapter Nine

On all previous occasions that he had used it the home dressing-room at Leeside Park had seemed to Mark to be a familiar and friendly place. Now, as kick-off time approached for the Liverpool match, the atmosphere was one of nervous tension and a sort of brooding trepidation. Hardly a single player appeared to be relaxed in any way. Conversations consisted of monosyllabic exchanges punctuated by long intervals.

Mark licked his lips for the umpteenth time and wished that Gareth Blake would hurry up and make an appearance. According to his team-mates, the manager always came in for a few words just before the players went out on to the park. It was an important ritual for the team, because invariably Blake succeeded in lifting morale.

The most familiar face belonged to Mason (usually known as Stoney) Smith, the former Scotland international and Athletic's longest-serving player. Usually he, like Mark, turned out for the Reserves, but because of the severe injury crisis he'd been recalled to the first team in the No. 11 shirt. Smith was fairly uncommunicative at the best of times but now he was plainly absorbed in his own thoughts. Once Mark caught his eye but all he was rewarded with was a half-grin. Mason was plotting the downfall of Liverpool in such a way that Gareth Blake would *have* to retain him in the side whatever the state of the first team's health.

Eventually Joe Landreth, another newcomer to the side, came across to Mark and asked him how he was feeling. Joe was a midfield player recently converted to the role of striker in the Reserves and he'd been given Jimmy Terndale's place for this match. To Mark, the fair haired Landreth seemed too slightly built for the harsh realities of life in the opposition's penalty area but so far he'd managed to take care of himself pretty well. Against Liverpool, however, his toughness and resilience would be tested to the full. With 9 as the number on his back the home crowd at least would expect him to lead the attack and challenge for everything that could be turned into a shooting chance.

'I've never felt so scared in my life,' Joe confessed in a whisper to Mark. 'I mean, suppose I miss a sitter with five minutes to go and still no score. The Boss and the fans'd never forgive me. They'd crucify me for not beating Liverpool. If only we were playing somebody like – oh, I don't know – Aldershot. I think I could just about cope with them!'

'Oh, I don't know,' Mark responded, somehow summoning up a smile and a cheerfulness he didn't really feel. 'If you missed a sitter against a side we were supposed to *murder* then they wouldn't forgive you. After all, the best strikers in Europe have failed to score against Liverpool. Anyway, Joe, at least you're *playing*. I reckon it'll be much worse for me having to sit and watch everything, not knowing if I'll have any chance of getting on.'

'Maybe you're right,' Joe conceded. 'I hope you're called on – though not,' he added hastily, 'in place of me!'

Mark felt a little easier knowing that someone else was suffering the same sort of fears. He'd seen very few instances of Joe's nervousness in the past so it had been a surprise to hear how worried the new striker was.

Then, to his amazement, a club official who'd come into the dressing-room announced, in a fairly loud voice, that one of the Liverpool players wanted to have a private word with Mark Fox as soon as possible.

That rather dramatic announcement had the immediate effect of deflating much of the tension that had been building up among the Athletic team. Inevitably, someone joked that the Liverpool lads must be wanting to bribe Athletic's sub to tell them all about the team's tactics for the match.

'Or maybe they're a player short and want to sign you up on instant registration forms, Mark!' cracked Ben Fitchfield, Athletic's skipper, who played in the midfield trio. 'So go and see 'em – but, remember, hold out for top terms. If Liverpool want the best, they've got to pay for 'em.'

'And see if you can pick up anything about *their* tactics!' Steve Walton, a back-four player, yelled after him as Mark slipped out of the dressing-room.

As soon as he spotted Tommy Archbold waiting in the corridor Mark knew he should have guessed who wanted to have a chat with him. He and Tommy had been team-mates with England Juniors and since then Tommy had gone from strength to strength. He had forced his way into the powerful Liverpool side by virtue of the goals he'd been regularly scoring in the Reserves in the Central League. In spite of his youth – and he wasn't much more than a year older than Mark – he was already being regarded as a fixture in the Reds' first team.

'Great to see you, wack!' Tommy greeted him with bubbling enthusiasm and a hearty slap on the shoulder. 'Knew you were going to make your mark – hey, great joke that, eh? – before long. Read all about you in the Liverpool paper last night. Made me think of the good times we had in Switzerland, wack! Great, there, wasn't it? So I hope you're going to have a good game today, Mark old mate, 's long as you don't put one over the Reds. Can't allow that, you know.'

Mark thought it was typical of Tommy's generous nature that he should seek an early opportunity to wish him well. The big Liverpool striker had never been one to stand on ceremony but not many young players would have had the nerve to ask to see an opponent for a private chat before the match at an away game.

After another few words and a promise to meet again if possible after the match, Mark returned to the dressing-room, only seconds ahead of Gareth Blake, who was coming in to wish his players luck. He looked more like a man who'd just been taking the chair at a meeting of international bankers. Certainly he seemed to dress for that part and on this occasion he was wearing a mid-blue worsted suit with a gold-and-black boldly striped tie.

'O.K., lads, there's nothing I can tell you that you don't already know,' he declared without any preliminaries. 'All I'll do is remind you that Liverpool, like any other team, are not invincible. We've defeated them before and we'll defeat them today as long as you keep your heads. They'll expect us to come out attacking because that's what home teams do. But our attacking will be at least twice as good as they expect. We'll attack and attack and attack until we're ready to drop. O.K.?'

Ricky Smith then moved in for a few final words with various individual players: and, five minutes later, the Athletic side clattered down the tunnel and out into the sunlight that was bathing Leeside Park. The crowd was bigger than any Mark had ever seen at the ground with the exception of the record-breaking figure that had turned up for an F.A. Cup-tie with Manchester United a few years earlier. The roar of the welcome from the home supporters was tremendous and Mark found it exhilarating: it made him wish, suddenly and deeply, that he was playing in the match. He wanted to be part of the excitement of a great occasion: for any match with a team like Liverpool *was* a great occasion.

He joined eagerly in the kick-in, first setting up shooting chances for Joe Landreth and Rob Youngman, two of the three main strikers, and then having a few cracks at goal himself. When he succeeded in putting the ball in the net a group of Liverpool supporters congregated at that end of the ground spontaneously chanted: 'You won't do that again, you won't do that again!' It brought a few laughs and jeers from Athletic fans.

Then, when the referee summoned the captains to the centre spot to toss up, Mark carried out the customary sub's duty of collecting track-suit tops from those who'd been wearing them. Even in such warm conditions one or two had kept them on simply because of a long-standing superstition. Mark delivered the kit to the dug-out – and then remembered that he'd promised to give a wave to his parents in the stand. He wasn't sure he'd be able to pick them out in such a sea of faces, though that hardly mattered. Now, however, that he'd forgotten to signal them he could do nothing about it: people would think he was crazy if he jumped up on to the touch-line and starting waving frantically at someone in the crowd! Perhaps they'd understand that he had too much on his mind to think about family obligations.

Liverpool won the toss and chose to play with the sun behind them; but they were pushed back on the defensive from the kick-off. Just as Gareth Blake had ordered, Athletic immediately stormed into the attack and put the Liverpool goal under siege. No doubt that was what the Reds had expected, but the ferocity and persistence of the home side's assault seemed to take them by surprise. They were given no time at all to settle down, to slow the game down and then, as they'd done so often all over England and Europe, dictate the course of the match.

Joe Landreth appeared to have overcome his worries very quickly and was zestfully combining with his co-striker, the tall and thin Rob Youngman, a former Celtic player and thus a close friend of Stoney Smith's. For his part, Stoney was leading the second wave of attackers instead of following his usual custom of controlling the left-side of midfield. As the Boss kept nodding his satisfaction every time Mason had the ball it was obvious to Mark that the former Scotland player was obeying new orders.

Nobody on the Liverpool side was feeling more frustrated than Tommy Archbold. He, of course, had expected to be leading the raids at the other end of the park and so, when he got tired of waiting for the ball to come to him, he went in search of it. His attempt to wrest it from Joe Landreth's control resulted in a free kick being awarded to Athletic. And from that kick, the home side very nearly scored.

Mason, a very precise placer of a ball in such situations, took the kick left-footed and floated it tantalisingly into the box so that the goalie was in a quandary about whether to come out for it or stay on his line. Rob Youngman went up for the ball, flicked it on cleverly and Joe Landreth produced an astounding overhead scissors kick to send the ball thudding against the angle of upright and crossbar. A Liverpool defender then took the sensible course of nodding the ball over the line for a corner.

The home crowd was now in great voice and baying for a goal. Within seconds, they nearly had one. Ben Fitchfield, the Athletic skipper, suddenly made a run from midfield, exchanged a swift one-two with Youngman, and then hit a shot from the edge of the box which the goalie had to go full-stretch to save by the post. Ben was elated with the outcome of his surge into attack: and, in the dug-out, Ricky Smith was semaphoring his own delight.

The tempo understandably dropped somewhat as half-time approached and the Reds even managed to break out of defence and set up an attack of their own. It was Tommy Archbold who wasted the chance when it came, shooting far too hurriedly and off-target. He had a good excuse, though: he'd been out of the game too long in terms of making contact with the ball.

There was one Athletic forward who'd seen very little of the ball, too: the electric right winger, Vic Church, one of the club's rising stars. So far all the attacks had emanated from the other flank because that was where Stoney Smith was operating. Now, however, a signal went out from the bench and, at the first opportunity, the ball was directed to the opposite wing.

Church's growing reputation as a fast and exceedingly tricky winger was well known to Liverpool and they'd been marking him closely. But because Church had so far been out of the action the marking had been relaxed a little, and that little turned out to be too much in the next few seconds. For Church, revelling in the space allowed him, took the ball right up to the by-line. Then, when challenged, he turned the Liverpool left-back, a Wales international, inside out to the roared approval of the crowd.

The penalty area was becoming crowded as Vic worked the ball along the line before, with a delicate and precise skill, lifting the ball into the middle. Once again Rob Youngman got his head to it, nodding it down for Joe Landreth to hurl himself at it. Joe was in almost a horizontal position as he made contact with the ball, glancing it just inside the right-hand upright.

By any standards, it was an exceptional – and brave – goal. The crowd erupted as Joe disappeared under a pile of team-mates eager to be the first to congratulate him on his debut goal. Gareth Blake, not normally an emotional man, was on his feet, leaping from the dug-out to join in the applause, along with Mark and the two coaches.

Only a minute later, however, the complexion of the game changed. Once more Joe Landreth was at the heart of things – but this time as the victim. Although Athletic tried to keep the pressure on Liverpool, a misplaced pass just outside the centre circle provided the Reds with a breakaway. A midfielder supplied Archbold with a superb pass and Tommy was just getting up steam when Joe, believing that the big striker would get clean away, lunged in with a desperate attempt at a tackle.

Tommy stumbled, tried to recover his momentum, failed and fell heavily right on top of the Athletic player. The referee, who'd just glanced at his watch, had no hesitation in calling for the trainer to come on. Joe was lying flat out and in obvious pain.

'Oh lord, not *another* serious injury!' groaned Gareth Blake as he, too, got to his feet.

Tommy watched with concern as Joe was carried on a stretcher from the pitch. But even Ben Fitchfield assured him that it was not his fault.

Mark, equally sickened by the disaster that had struck Athletic, couldn't help wondering just what effect it would have on his own position. He moistened his lips at the thought that any moment now he might be pitched headlong into the match. It was what he'd dreamed about for years, prayed for, even; but now that he was on the very edge of that experience of a lifetime he suddenly felt dreadfully nervous. Would he make a complete hash of his first kick of the ball? Would he play so badly that the crowd would boo his efforts? Yet, in the same moment, he knew that he was eager to get his chance to prove that he *could* play: that he was fast and skilful and nerveless in the most exciting place of all, the opposition's penalty area.

The Boss, however, was giving nothing away of his intentions. In any case, as it was so close to the interval he had no need to send on his substitute. Joe might not be badly hurt and thus able to resume after half-time. So Mark tried not to think about his own fate. In recent times he'd been accused of a lack of loyalty to his team. Well, he wasn't going to allow that to occur again. Deliberately he thought about someone else: Albie Jones. He tried to imagine how Albie might be getting on in that afternoon's Zenith League game. It might even be his last for Watchford because Buzz Burton had promised Mark that Albie could have a trial with Athletic. Knowing Albie, he'd make the most of that opportunity.

Next instant, the half-time whistle shrilled, and Mark was jerked back to the present.

During the interval there was again a subdued air in the home dressing-room in spite of the fact that Athletic were still winning 1-0. Joe's injury had upset everyone and the feeling was that it might well disturb the rhythm of the team in the second half. Apart from congratulating the players on their performance, Gareth Blake had little time to spend with them: he wanted to get the earliest possible news of Joe's medical condition. So it was Ricky Smith who dispensed confidence-boosting comments to individual players along with the cups of tea and slices of orange.

When the second half started it was, predictably, Liverpool who launched the first offensive. The Boss was missing from the dug-out, Athletic were playing only ten men and Mark still had no idea whether he was going to be called on. But Liverpool's determined raid fizzled out because of some deft footwork from Steve Walton, the rapidly improving right-back Athletic had signed from non-League football before the start of the season. Ben Fitchfield, who was having a fine all round game, sent Rob Youngman off on a mazy run: but without Joe Landreth to give support, nothing came of it. Mark desperately wanted to ask Ricky Smith what would happen if Joe didn't resume but he desisted. He'd learn soon enough.

Then, six minutes into the half with the game revolving round midfield, Gareth Blake returned. Tersely he told Ricky that Joe had gone off to hospital for precautionary X-rays, though it was thought the trouble was no more than deep bruising. Then he turned to Mark.

'Right, son, better get warmed up on the touchline,' he said briskly. 'We're going to need you.'

A few moments later, following a stoppage in play, the referee's attention was attracted by Ricky Smith and Mark Fox went on to the pitch to play his first game in the First Division for Athletic F.C. In those seconds before he actually crossed the touchline his mouth was dry with apprehension. But Gareth Blake had made the thoughtful gesture of standing beside him. And, when Mark moved off, the words that were in his ears were the Manager's: 'Go on and do your best, Mark. That'll be good enough for me.'

Almost as soon as he took up his position on Rob Youngman's right to assume Joe Landreth's role, Mark was involved in the game – and with his first kick his worries vanished. The ball was pushed through smartly by Ben Fitchfield, Rob flicked it on intelligently and Mark reacted fast to take it in his stride and steer it wide of a challenging Liverpool midfielder.

Using his quicksilver acceleration to dramatic effect, Mark surged away again and then changed direction to move out to the right flank. That manoeuvre took even some of his colleagues by surprise because Mark was principally a left-footed player. Then Mark dummied neatly past a Liverpool back-four player and looked up: he spotted Rob Youngman sprinting for the edge of the box. With a perfectly judged chip, Mark sent him the ball. Rob moved to meet it, controlled it superbly and hit a screamer of a shot which the Reds' goalie was exceedingly fortunate to turn over the bar with his fingertips.

The sequence of play since Mark first touched the

ball had been so swift and successful that the home crowd treated their players to a prolonged burst of cheering and clapping. With the exception of Joe's goal, it was the most exhilarating moment in the match to date. Mark Fox had shown them that he had the right instinct: to attack.

'Great start, keep it up, Mark!' Ben said to him, slapping him on the back as the players took up their positions for the resultant corner kick.

Rob, too, had indicated his appreciation of the way Mark had supplied the ball for that shot on the turn. Mark's confidence soared. He hadn't expected to touch the ball in the first few minutes, let alone make such a significant contribution to Athletic's attack. For their part, Liverpool plainly were taken aback by Mark Fox's pace and his close control. From now on, he was going to get the sort of close marking that any brilliant opponent warranted.

The corner kick was punched clear by a grateful goalkeeper. Mark retreated hurriedly and bumped into Tommy Archbold. 'Hey, did you a good turn when I clobbered your No. 9 and got you into the match instead, didn't I?' chortled Tommy, irrepressible as ever. Mark merely grinned.

Five minutes later, Tommy had cause to congratulate himself again: this time, though, his contribution to the match was definitely in favour of Liverpool. A very long kick out of defence was completely, and inexplicably, missed by Athletic's centre-back. It was his first and only mistake of the game but Liverpool made a habit of punishing cardinal errors. In a trice Tommy Archbold was in possession and, with a stunning change of pace and then a body swerve, he sped past the next defender and into the penalty area. Roger Tandy, Athletic's goalkeeper, hesitated fractionaly about coming out. But that didn't really make any difference. Tommy simply hit the ball with all the power he possessed and it flew, rocket-like, into the top corner of the net, giving Roger no hope at all of saving it.

It was exactly the kind of goal that had earned Tommy his reputation as one of the First Division's most exciting young players. He was ecstatic – and so were his team-mates – but no one in the Liverpool side was prepared to regard a draw as a satisfactory reward. For their part, Athletic were equally determined to regain the lead. So, for the next few minutes, the match was played at a furious pace with chances being created at both ends: only to be stifled by good defensive work or acrobatic goalkeeping. The crowd, of course, were revelling in the excitement.

When the news, signalled from the bench, reached Mark that only about two minutes of the match remained he was astonished: he had never known time disappear so quickly. The Boss was demanding an all-out attack to wrest two points from the match instead of one – and the midfield responded magnificently. Ben seized possession in a tussle for the ball with his Liverpool counterpart, and then darted for space. Vic Church, who'd come inside to make a tactical switch, played a one-two with his skipper; and then the ball was fired through a narrow gap with great precision to reach Rob Youngman, loitering with intent on the far corner of the penalty area. Without a split-second's hesitation, he back-heeled the ball fiercely towards Mark Fox – and the Reds' defence was taken completely by surprise.

Mark's initial acceleration was breathtaking. Then, with a tilt of one shoulder, he fooled a defender into thinking he was going left instead of right, and burst into the box. Already the goalkeeper was advancing – and now, as Mark started to swerve round him, he dived to try and smother the ball. Mark pushed the ball out of the goalie's reach and was about to slide it into the empty net when the keeper caught his ankle and sent Mark tumbling over and over.

The huge roar from the crowd for 'Penalty!' was answered by the referee practically before the sound reached him. His finger was pointing melodramatically towards the spot as Mark ruefully picked himself up, only to be deluged with congratulations by his team-mates. From the crowd the cheering was loud and prolonged.

'Great effort, Mark, great effort!' Ben told him for the second time in the match.

With the final seconds of the match ticking away, Mason Smith strolled up to take the kick as if there were all the time in the world at his disposal. In any case, he knew that a referee always had to add time on for a penalty kick if necessary. Then, with a remarkable combination of nonchalance, precision and power, the old warrior struck the ball superbly into the net by the foot of the right-hand upright for the winning goal. Moments later, while the players were still on their way to take up their formations again, the final whistle shrilled.

As the teams left the pitch Mason Smith made a point

of having a word with Mark, who was just beginning to realise what a great match it had been for him, even if he hadn't scored the goal he felt he'd deserved.

'That run of yours deserved the goal, laddie,' the former international told him. 'But ye'll be scoring your first for this club before long, I've nae doot about that. I reckon ye'll go a long way in this game.'